LENIN
on the JEWISH QUESTION

LENIN

on the
JEWISH
QUESTION

Edited by Hyman Lumer

INTERNATIONAL PUBLISHERS, New York

© International Publishers Co. Inc., 1974
All Rights Reserved
First Edition, 1974

Library of Congress Cataloging in Publication Data

Lenin, Vladimir Il'ich, 1870-1924.
Lenin on the Jewish question.

1. Jews in Russia—Political and social conditions.
2. Nationalism—Jews. 3. Ogólny Zydowski Związek
robotniczy "Bund" na Litwie, w Polsce i w Rosji.
I. Title.
DS135.R9L373   323.1′19′24047   74-6278
ISBN 0-7178-0398-8
ISBN 0-7178-0399-6 (pbk.)

CONTENTS

LENIN
on the JEWISH QUESTION

INTRODUCTION

Among V. I. Lenin's most outstanding theoretical contributions are his writings on the national question. That he dealt extensively with this subject is not surprising, in the "prisonhouse of nations" that was tsarist Russia liberation of the oppressed nations and national minorities and unification of workers of diverse nationalities against their common oppressor were in the forefront of the problems faced by the revolutionary movement. Within this context the Jewish question occupies a prominent position, first, because the Jews were, as Lenin notes, the most oppressed of all nationalities in tsarist Russia, and second, because of the lengthy battle that had to be waged against the nationalist stand of the Jewish Bund (the General Jewish Workers' Union in Lithuania, Poland and Russia), which called for a separate political organization for Jewish workers and claimed the sole right to speak for them.

However, Lenin dealt with the Jewish question not in isolation but as an important component of the national question as a whole. He wrote no special treatises on the Jewish question as such. Rather, his references to it occur mainly within his writings on the national question in general and particularly in his numerous polemics against the Bund, whose separatism was an obstacle to the building of the Russian Social-Democratic Labor Party as a party of *all* workers in tsarist Russia. Indeed, many of Lenin's most important theoretical contributions are to be found in these polemics.

Consequently, a compilation of Lenin's writings on the Jewish question must of necessity include a substantial body of material on the national question as a whole, as well as considerable repetition of certain points to which Lenin had to return repeatedly in the fight against the nationalism of the Bund. What we have sought to do in this volume is to present a comprehensive selection of Lenin's writings on the subject within the context in which they were written, though without pretending to literal completeness. The selections are taken from the English edition of the *Collected Works*, issued by Progress Publishers in Moscow between 1960 and 1970, and are presented in the order in which they appear there. An appendix presents two important documents implementing Lenin's policies following the October Revolution.

* * *

Lenin's approach to the Jewish question, as to the national question in general, was a consistently class approach. Its point of departure was the need to unite workers of all nationalities against the tsarist autocracy and the capitalist class, which sought to divide them along national lines. In particular, he fought unceasingly for unity of Jewish and non-Jewish workers and against the anti-Semitism which was a prime weapon of the ruling class for splitting the workers and turning them against one another.

As early as 1903, on the occasion of the Second Congress of the RSDLP, he noted that "the fullest and closest unity of the militant proletariat is absolutely essential both for the purpose of achievement of its ultimate aim and in the interests of an unswerving political and economic struggle in conditions of the existing society." And he added that "in particular, complete unity between the Jewish and non-Jewish proletariat is moreover especially necessary for a successful struggle against anti-Semitism, this despicable attempt of the government and the exploiting classes to exacerbate racial particularism and national enmity." (P. 26.)

The theme of international working-class unity runs like a red thread through all of Lenin's writings. And he continually inveighs against bourgeois nationalism as an ideology which divides the working class. Thus, in 1913 he writes:

The class-conscious workers combat *all* national oppression and *all* national privileges, but they do not confine themselves to that. They combat all, even the most refined nationalism and advocate not only the unity but also the *amalgamation* of the workers of all nationalities in the struggle against reaction and against bourgeois nationalism in all its forms. Our task is not to segregate nations, but to unite the workers of all nations. Our banner does not carry the slogan "national culture" but *international* culture, which unites all the nations in a higher,

socialist unity, and the way to which is already being paved by
the international amalgamation of capital. (Pp. 98-99.)

Unity and amalgamation. These concepts were fundamental in
Lenin's thinking. And from this standpoint he fought tirelessly to
unite the workers of the diverse nationalities in tsarist Russia, to
bring them together in a single movement, a single working-class
revolutionary party. He clashed uncompromisingly with
nationalists of all stripes and the nationalism they preached, and in
particular with the Bund.

This nationalist organization was formed as a separate revolutionary party for Jewish workers, independently determining its own
policies and joining with the RSDLP on a basis of federation. It
claimed for itself the status of sole representative of the Jewish
revolutionary workers and insisted that within such a federated relationship as it proposed the RSDLP could address the Jewish
workers only through its intermediacy.

To this proposal to isolate the Jewish workers from those of other
nationalities and thus to weaken the whole struggle against tsarist
autocracy and capitalist exploitation, Lenin counterposed the concept of a unitary working-class party based on the principle of
democratic centralism. This "party of a new type" was a party with
a single program and policy, democratically determined but bind-
ing, once agreed upon, on all subordinate bodies and individual
members. As against federation, Lenin posed the concept of autonomy of party organizations representing specific groups of
workers with regard to forms and methods of carrying out party
policy within their particular fields of operation. Only such a united, disciplined party, Lenin contended, could effectively lead the
struggles of the working class and the toiling masses. And indeed it
was just such a party which led the workers and peasants to victory
in the October Revolution.

The checkered career of the Bund—splitting from the RSDLP in
1903, rejoining it in 1906, later splitting again and ultimately sink-
ing into Menshevism and counterrevolution—is amply set forth in
Lenin's writings and the accompanying notes presented in this
volume.

But the differences with the Bund were not purely on organizational questions. On the contrary, the organizational disputes
stemmed from underlying ideological differences. The Bund's posi-

tion was based not on proletarian internationalism but on Jewish nationalism. Though it declared itself to be opposed to Zionism it nevertheless borrowed from Zionist precepts. It grasped, said Lenin, "at the idea of a Jewish '*nation*' " (p. 39). But, Lenin maintained, "this Zionist idea is absolutely false and essentially reactionary" (*ibid.*). Lacking even a common territory and a common language, the Jews could in no sense be considered a nation. He added: "Absolutely untenable scientifically, the idea that the Jews form a separate nation is reactionary politically." (P. 48.) The Bund's position was helping "not to end but to increase and legitimize Jewish isolation, by propagating the idea of a Jewish 'nation' and a plan for federating Jewish and non-Jewish proletarians." (P. 49.) It served to perpetuate, not to end the tsarist ghettoization of Jews.

*   *   *

The legitimizing of Jewish isolation was fostered particularly by the Bund's advocacy of "cultural-national autonomy." This idea was a natural outgrowth of the notion that the Jews, though lacking a common territory, constitute a nation. It was noteworthy, Lenin pointed out, that its only exponents in Russia were the Jewish bourgeois parties and the Bund. In the absence of a common territory their separatism could only take the form of demands for *extraterritorial* autonomy.

According to this concept every individual, regardless of place of residence, would be permitted to register as a member of a given nation. More specifically any Jew, whether living in Moscow, Kiev, Vilna or Tbilisi, could register as a member of an extraterritorial Jewish "nation." Such a "nation" would constitute a legal entity with powers to tax, to elect a national parliament and to appoint ministers. But these would operate within the framework of the tsarist autocracy and their jurisdiction would be limited to cultural affairs.

Since education is a central aspect of cultural affairs, the essence of this scheme, said Lenin, is that it "ensures absolute precision and absolute consistency in segregating the schools according to nationality." (P. 88.) Such segregation, he contended, could serve only to divide workers of different nationalities. In the case of the Jews, already confined to ghettos and denied access to Russian schools, it could only mean perpetuation of their isolation and the discrimination imposed on them. Separate schools for Jews was the slogan of the forces of tsarist reaction; it was with these forces, Lenin warned, that the Bund was allying itself.

The slogan of cultural-national autonomy is rooted, he said, in the bourgeois-nationalist concept of a nonclass "national culture." "The slogan of national culture," he wrote, "is a bourgeois)and often also a Black-Hundred and clerical) fraud. Our slogan is: the international culture of democracy and of the world working-class movement." (P. 104.) There are, he asserted, in every capitalist country *two* cultures:

> The *elements* of democratic and socialist culture are present, if only in rudimentary form, in *every* national culture, since in *every* nation there are toiling and exploited masses, whose conditions inevitably give rise to the ideology of democracy and socialism. But *every* nation also possesses a bourgeois culture (and most nations a reactionary and clerical culture as well) in the form, not merely of "elements," but of the *dominant* culture. Therefore the general "national culture" *is* the culture of the landlords, the clergy and the bourgeoisie. This fundamental and, for a Marxist, elementary truth, was in fact kept in the background by the Bundist. . . . *In fact*, the Bundist acted like a bourgeois, whose every interest requires the spreading of a belief in a non-class national culture. (P. 105.)

But "international culture is not non-national." It is not a culture in which all national differences are obliterated. On the contrary, says Lenin: "In advancing the slogan of 'the international culture of democracy and of the working-class movement,' we take *from each* national culture *only* its democratic and socialist elements; we take them *only* and *absolutely* in opposition to the bourgeois culture and the bourgeois nationalism of *each* nation." (P. 105.) This approach serves to unite workers of different nationalities, whereas the slogan of "national culture" serves to divide them and to tie the workers of each nationality to its "own" bourgeoisie. Lenin adds:

> The same applies to the most oppressed and persecuted nation—the Jews. Jewish national culture is the slogan of the rabbis and the bourgeoisie, the slogan of our enemies. But there are other elements in Jewish culture and in Jewish history as a whole. Of the ten and a half million Jews in the world,

somewhat over a half live in Galicia and Russia, backward and semi-barbarous countries, where the Jews are *forcibly* kept in the status of a caste. The other half lives in the civilized world, where the Jews do not live as a segregated caste. There the great world-progressive features of Jewish culture stand clearly revealed: its internationalism, its identification with the advanced movements of the epoch (the percentage of Jews in the democratic and proletarian movements is everywhere higher than the percentage of Jews among the population). (P. 107.)

In rejecting cultural-national autonomy, Lenin maintained that autonomy can only be *territorial* in character. That is, it can be exercised only where people of a given nationality inhabit a common territory. For nations, freedom from national oppression means exercise of the right of self-determination—the right to secede and form a separate state. But for national groups living within the territory of other nations it can mean only the attainment of consistent democracy, of full equality. "Social-democrats," wrote Lenin, "in upholding a consistently democratic state system, demand unconditional equality for all nationalities and struggle against absolutely all privileges for one or several nationalities." (P. 77.)

But he never lost sight of the class context within which this demand is raised. In contrast to the bourgeoisie, he stressed, the basic concern of workers is not the preservation of national distinctions but rather the drawing together of the workers of all nationalities.

* * *

This brings us to the subject of Lenin's views on assimilation, which have been particularly subjected to distortion by bourgeois critics and by certain erstwhile Jewish Marxists infected with bourgeois nationalism.

Lenin, it is said, based himself on the since discredited writings of Karl Kautsky, who saw the distinctive features of Jews as the product of their persecution and isolation. With these ended they would simply be absorbed into the societies in which they lived and disappear as a distinct national group. And this, Kautsky argued, would be a desirable outcome since the Yiddish language

and the culture based on it were only products of forced ghettoization.*

In accepting this idea, it is maintained, Lenin was wrong. As
some put it, Lenin joined in the error of failing to recognize that
other factors besides anti-Semitism and ghettoization were responsible for, the continued existence of the Jews as a distinct
nationality—religious, historical and cultural factors. And when
Lenin posed the alternatives for the Jewish people as isolation or
assimilation, they add, he failed to foresee that history would provide another alternative—that of integration.

Moreover, it is said, Lenin could not have foreseen such developments as the Hitlerite slaughter of Jews or the founding of
the State of Israel, both of which have been powerful forces in
perpetuating Jewish national consciousness. Had he lived longer, it
is implied, he would have modified his views.

But this is a vulgarization of Lenin's ideas. True, he cites
Kautsky on the assimilation of the Jewish people, but his views are
no mere parroting of Kautsky. On the contrary, Lenin's own
theoretical treatment of the question goes far beyond that of
Kautsky. Unlike Kautsky's, Lenin's approach is a thoroughly
dialectical one.

Lenin conceived of amalgamation in terms not merely of assimilation of national minorities but of the eventual fusion of *nations*.
This, he contended, grows out of the very historical process that
gave rise to nations in the first place. The modern nation arose
with the development of capitalism, of a system of commodity production whose functioning demanded the amalgamation of the
smaller feudal communities. But the growing economic interdependence which led to the emergence of nations and nation-
states did not stop at national boundaries. The development of
capitalism led to the rise of a world economy, marked by growing
intercourse and interdependence between nation. And this

---

* Over a period of years Kautsky wrote a number of articles on the subject. His
main work, the book *Rasse und Judentum (Race and Jewry)* appeared in 1914. A
revised German edition was published in 1921 and this, with further updating, was
published in English translation in 1926 by International Publishers, New York,
under the title *Are the Jews a Race?*

brought with it the progressive breaking down of national barriers
and national exclusiveness.

Thus, Lenin saw two historical tendencies in operation. In the
much-quoted passage from his "Critical Remarks on the National
Question" he says:

> Developing capitalism knows two historical tendencies in the
> national question. The first is the awakening of national life and
> national movements, the struggle against all national oppression
> and the creation of national states. The second is the develop-
> ment and the growing frequency of international intercourse in
> every form, the breakdown of national barriers, the creation of
> the international unity of capital, of economic life in general, of
> politics, science, etc.

> Both tendencies are a universal law of capitalism. The former
> predominates in the beginning of its development, the latter
> characterizes a mature capitalism that is moving towards its
> transformation into socialist society. (P. 108.)

Lenin asks: "Is there anything real left in the concept of assimilation, after all violence and all inequality are eliminated?" And he
replies: "Yes, there undoubtedly is. What is left is capitalism's
world-historical tendency to break down national barriers, obliterate national distinctions, and to *assimilate* nations—a tendency
which manifests itself with every passing decade, and is one of the
greatest driving forces transforming capitalism into socialism." (P.
109.)

Note that Lenin speaks of a "world-historical tendency" to "assimilate nations." More, he views this tendency not as coming into
operation *after* the ending of national oppression but as existing
simultaneously with the opposing tendency, that expressed in the
striving for national freedom, national equality and national identity. He treats the two opposing tendencies as a dialectical unity of
opposites and the contradiction between them as the motive force
of national evolution. In this process, he says, it is the tendency
toward assimilation that represents the future and must be recognized as a progressive tendency. It was in this light that he viewed
the assimilation of national minorities and particularly that of the
Jews.

For capitalism the two tendencies present an irreconcilable contradiction, since capitalism knows no relationship other then that

based on exploitation and national oppression for the sake of capitalist profits. It is this aim which is served by the ideology of chauvinism and racism, including anti-Semitism. It is only in a socialist society, Lenin maintained, that such barriers to amalgamation can be fully removed. For him the fight against national oppression, though absolutely essential, was never one for the perpetuation of national distinctions; its goal was rather to pave the way for the free, voluntary union of peoples as equals.

He recognized the amalgamation of nations and national groups into broader communities as a feature of the socialist and communist future, as a development to be welcomed. The proletariat, he said, supports everything that helps to do away with national isolation, to create closer ties between nationalities, to merge nations, while at the same time he recognized that the basis of this process lies in uncompromising struggle against all forms of national oppression.

In the case of the Jewish people he notes that

. . . it is only Jewish reactionary philistines, who want to turn back the wheel of history, and make it proceed, not from the conditions prevailing in Russia and Galicia to those prevailing in Paris and New York, but in the reverse direction—only they can clamor against "assimilation."

The best Jews, those who are celebrated in world history, and have given the world foremost leaders of democracy and socialism, have never clamored against assimilation. It is only those who contemplate the "rear aspect" of Jewry with reverential awe that clamor against assimilation. (P. 110.)

* * *

These words are no less true today than when Lenin wrote them. It is the Zionists—the purveyors of extreme Jewish nationalism and separatism—who lead the fight against assimilation and for the preservation of "Jewish identity." And in their view this means precisely what Lenin refers to as "the culture of the rabbis and the bourgeoisie." It means especially the preservation of the Jewish religion and in particular, among Soviet Jews, of Orthodox Judaism. To them the measure of "Jewish identity" in the Soviet Union is the number of synagogues, rabbis, prayer shawls and phylacteries. To them the dwindling number of practicing believers is a sign of cultural genocide.

Undoubtedly the day will ultimately come when there is not one synagogue (or church or mosque) left in the Soviet Union. Will this mean that the Soviet Jewish people have suffered cultural genocide? Not at all. What it *will* mean is that they, like other Soviet citizens, have advanced beyond adherence to religious superstition, that they no longer have any use for religious institutions and practices, that religious distinctions between Jews and non-Jews have vanished. But to Zionism, which equates "Jewish identity" with Judaism, this is a calamity.

Similarly, the day will come when Yiddish will have disappeared as a spoken language. Will this, too, mean that Soviet Jews have suffered cultural genocide? Not at all. Languages have their own process of historical evolution. It will simply mean that, living as equals among other people and freely intermingling with them, they will no longer have need of a separate language and least of all will they have need of segregated schools taught in that language. But the Zionists (who themselves for the most part do not speak Yiddish, and in Israel regard Hebrew as the language of the Jewish people) clamor for the preservation of Yiddish—in the Soviet Union—as the essence of Jewish culture and the hallmark of "Jewish identity." In this respect, too, they look toward the past, not the future.

Lenin wrote that "those Jewish Marxists who mingle with the Russian, Lithuanian, Ukrainian and other workers in international Marxist organizations, and make their contribution (both in Russian and in Yiddish) towards creating the international culture of the working-class movement—those Jews, despite the separatism of the Bund, uphold the best traditions of Jewry by fighting the slogan of 'national culture.' " (P. 107.)

This concept of "creating the international culture of the working-class movement" is central in the historical development of the USSR, where the abolition of national discrimination has given birth to a new kind of historical community, the *Soviet* people, embracing the myriad nations and nationalities within the Soviet state. In the words of Leonid Brezhnev, general secretary of the CPSU Central Committee:

A new historical community of people, the Soviet people, took shape in our country during the years of socialist construction. New, harmonious relations, relations of friendship and

> cooperation, were formed between the classes and social
> groups, nations and nationalities in joint labor, in the struggle
> for socialism, and in the battles fought in defense of socialism.
> Our people are welded together by a common Marxist-Leninist
> ideology and the lofty aims of building communism. *(Report of
> the CPSU Central Committee to the 24th Congress of the CPSU,*
> Novosti Press Agency Publishing House, Moscow, 1971, p. 90.)

The Soviet Jews are an intimate part of this new historical community. Though offered the opportunity to establish a separate
Jewish Autonomous Region in Birobidjan, few of them chose this
path. The removal of all restrictions on Jews after the October Revolution led them not to Birobidjan but to Moscow, Leningrad,
Kiev and other urban centers where they took advantage of the
opportunity to enter industry and the professions. The overwhelming majority of Soviet Jews have, in fact, come to look upon themselves simply as Soviet citizens, as an integral part of the Soviet
people.

There are, it is true, some negative influences of the past, expressed in part in the migration of a certain number of Soviet Jews
to Israel. But such influences affect only a small minority. Soviet
Jews on the whole emphatically reject them.

They are an intimate part of the unification of peoples and cultures taking place in the Soviet Union today, a development possible only in a socialist society in which the class and national antagonisms generated by capitalist exploitation and oppression have
been abolished and in which there is a harmony of the interests of
all the people. Of this the well-known Soviet scholar, Professor
Iosef Braginsky, editor-in-chief of *Narody Azii i Afriki (Peoples of
Asia and Africa),* himself Jewish, writes:

> The Marxist cannot view Jewish assimilation from the narrow
> angle of "dos pintele yid" [the Jewish spark]. One has to realize
> that assimilation is a natural, historical process. In the USSR
> assimilation is taking place in conditions of friendship among the
> peoples and national equality. National consolidation and inter-
> national integration represent two sides of the development of
> one Soviet nation, which is inspired by feelings of Soviet na-
> tional pride. *(Once Again About Assimilation,* Novosti Press
> Agency, Moscow, October 1964.)

Here we witness in actual process the "amalgamation of nations" of which Lenin wrote. What is envisaged is that with the full flowering of communism will come the full unity of all Soviet peoples. In the words of the *Program of the CPSU:*

> Full-scale communist construction constitutes a new stage in the development of national relations in the USSR in which the nations will draw still closer together until complete unity is achieved. The building of the material and technical basis of communism leads to still greater unity of the Soviet peoples. The exchange of material and spiritual values between nations becomes more and more intensive, and the contribution of each republic to the common cause of communist construction increases. Obliteration of distinctions between classes and the development of communist social relations make for a still greater social homogeneity of nations and contribute to the development of common communist traits in their culture, morals and way of living, to a further strengthening of their mutual trust and friendship. (International Publishers, New York, 1963, p. 116.)

What is envisaged is that ultimately national distinctions, like class distinctions, will vanish. The full realization of this, as Lenin makes clear, is seen as a matter of the as yet distant future. But the process leading toward that outcome is taking place now and its effects are already clearly visible.

Moreover, Lenin's concept of assimilation is not one of the simple absorption of one nationality by another, of the literal disappearance of national groups. On the contrary, as we have already noted, he stresses that the international culture of the working class which he advocates is not non-national but brings together what is progressive and democratic in each national culture. And in the case of the Jews he writes that "in the civilized world, where the Jews do not live as a segregated caste . . . the great world-progressive features of Jewish culture stand revealed: its internationalism, its identification with the advanced movements of the epoch. . . ."

National consciousness and national pride are not obliterated. Rather there develop mutual respect and friendship, and with this a growing intermingling of cultures. Such is Lenin's dialectical approach to the question of assimilation, whose validity the experience of the Soviet Union is bearing out.

* * *

Lenin was an indefatigable opponent of anti-Semitism. The Jews, he said, were the most oppressed of all peoples in tsarist Russia. And they were the chief victims of the efforts of the tsarist autocracy to divert the wrath of the people from itself by turning one group against another through the stirring up of racial and national animosity. These efforts were intensified with the rise of the revolutionary movement and were expressed in a wave of pogroms beginning in 1903. He saw clearly the class roots of this persecution. He said:

> It is not the Jews who are the enemies of the working people. The enemies of the workers are the capitalists of all countries. Among the Jews there are working people, and they form the majority. They are our brothers, who, like us, are oppressed by capital; they are our comrades in the struggle for socialism. Among the Jews there are kulaks, exploiters and capitalists, just as there are among Russians, and among people of all nations. . . . Rich Jews, like rich Russians, and the rich of all countries, are in alliance to oppress, crush, rob and disunite the workers. (pp. 135-136.)

In characterizing anti-Semitism as the instrument of the ruling class to divide the workers, Lenin clashed from the outset with the Bund, which viewed it as rooted in the masses of non-Jewish workers as well as in the bourgeoisie and the tsarist autocracy. In its stand, he charged, the Bund acted to blunt the class consciousness of the Jewish workers and to encourage the Zionist fable that anti-Semitism is eternal (pp. 22-24).

In the fight for national equality, Lenin gave first place to combatting the oppression of the Jewish people. Thus, a bill introduced in the Duma on this question in 1914 is entitled "A Bill for the Abolition of All Disabilities of the Jews and of All Restrictions on the Grounds of Origin or Nationality" (p. 125). The reason for putting it this way, said Lenin, was obvious: no nationality was so oppressed as the Jews, and anti-Semitism played a special role in the efforts of the ruling class to split the workers.

On the very heels of the October Revolution came the Declaration of the Rights of the Nationalities of Russia, presented in the

Appendix of this volume, which proclaimed the equality, sovereignty and right of self-determination of all nations of Russia and called for the abolition of all national privilege and discrimination. For the Jews this meant the almost overnight removal of the scores of anti-Semitic restrictions which had plagued them and the establishment of full freedom and equality. This was a truly remarkable achievement, comparable in magnitude and significance to what would be achieved in the United States if all racist practices and all forms of discrimination against the Black and other oppressed peoples were totally abolished. It is a glowing tribute to Lenin's grasp of the national question and an important component of the resolution of the national question in the socialist Soviet Union, one of its most outstanding achievements.

In the period of civil war which followed the October Revolution it was the counterrevolutionary forces (whom the Zionists and Bundists generally supported) that resorted to pogroms and other anti-Semitic acts. These were energetically fought by the revolutionary forces as the Resolution of the Council of People's Commissars on the Uprooting of the Anti-Semitic Movement (pp. 141-142) indicates. This resolution was the outcome of a report to Lenin by the newly established Commissar for Jewish Affairs, Shimen Dimanshtein, who wrote that when he informed Lenin of these anti-Semitic manifestations the latter was furious and called at once for the sharpest countermeasures. Such were Lenin's reactions to the crime of anti-Semitism at all times.

The result of Lenin's policy on the Jewish question was, as is well known, a flourishing of Jewish culture in the years following the revolution. Schools, newspapers, magazines, books and theaters in the Yiddish language multiplied. In addition, Birobidjan in eastern Siberia was declared a Jewish Autonomous Region for those Jews who might wish to establish a community of their own.

But the liberation of the Russian Jews led to precisely what Lenin had predicted: a rapid development of the process of assimilation. Freed from confinement to the poverty-stricken ghetto villages they poured into the large cities where they found employment in industry and other occupations. No longer excluded from Russian schools they flocked into them as the gateway to the learned professions.

In his *Pictorial History of the Jewish People*, Nathan Ausubel writes, after describing Yiddish cultural activities in the Soviet Union in the twenties and thirties:

> Yet, for all this unprecedented, large-scale Yiddish cultural activity, its decline was already in evidence at the very time of its flowering. Although hundreds of thousands of Soviet Jewish youth had been raised in Yiddish-language schools, the political and cultural pressures from without proved well-nigh irresistible. . . .
>
> In time, there was a sharp decline in the attendance of the Yiddish-language schools . . . the youth turned more and more to reading Russian newspapers, periodicals and books. In a late census, before the nazi attack on Russia, more Jews claimed Russian than Yiddish as their mother tongue. (Crown, New York, 1958, p. 253.)

This process was distorted for a time by the arbitrary closing down of Jewish cultural institutions by the Stalin regime and by the inclusion of many leading Jewish cultural figures among the victims of Stalin's crimes. But it has nevertheless taken its inexorable course. In the latest census only me 17 per cent of Soviet Jews claimed Yiddish as their mother tongue. The demand for Yiddish-language cultural institutions has greatly dwindled. And the Jewish religion, like others, is fast dying out.

There remains, to be sure, an appreciable though declining interest in Yiddi h language culture. This is attested to by the existence of the monthly literary magazine *Sovetish Heimland* with a circulation of 25,000, by the existence of a number of Yiddish theatrical groups, by Yiddish music concerts, by the continuing publication of books in Yiddish and by the publication of the newspaper *Birobidjaner Shtern*, which appears four times a week. But it must be stressed that this is a limited and declining interest.

Does this mean that Jewish culture is disappearing? Not at all. On the contrary, the best of it is becoming a part of the total Soviet cultural heritage. The works of the Yiddish classicists Sholem Aleichem, Y. L. Peretz and Mendele Mocher Sforim are published in ˙voluminous editions in Russian and other languages and are widely read. The same is true of other leading Jewish novelists and poets. Jewish culture is becoming part of the over-all cultural life of the Soviet people.

To be sure, the Yiddish language and Yiddish-language culture

will endure for some time to come and the distinctive existence of
the Jews for a much longer period. But the basic historical trend,
as Lenin defined it, is unmistakable. There is no third alternative
of "integration" as some maintain, unless one wishes merely to
substitute this term for assimilation.

The present-day nationalist correctors of Lenin contend that historical developments since World Was I have basically altered the
process. The past several decades, they say, have witnessed a
flowering of nations and a growth of national consicousness, national pride and national cultures rather than a process of national
diminution and amalgamation. And this is evident among the
Jewish people, the Soviet Jews included, no less than among
others.

Had Lenin lived longer, they maintain, he would have modified
his views accordingly; indeed, after the October Revolution he had
already begun to do so. The principal evidence for this contention
is the following quotation from his *"Left-Wing" Communism*:

> . . . As long as national and state distinctions exist among peo-
> ples and countries—and these will continue to exist for a long
> time to come, even after the dictatorship of the proletariat has
> been established on a world-wide scale—the unity of the inter-
> national tactics of the Communist working-class movement in all
> countries demands, not the elimination of variety or the sup-
> pression of national distinctions (which is a pipe dream at pres-
> ent), but the application of the *fundamental* principles of Com-
> munism (Soviet power and the dictatorship of the proletariat),
> which *correctly modify* these principles in certain *particulars,*
> correctly adapt and apply them to national and national-state
> distinctions. (*Collected Works,* Vol. 31, p. 92.)

This is often accompanied by reference to Lenin's strictures on the
need for extreme sensitivity to the feelings of oppressed peoples.
But as we have shown above, these later statements by Lenin represent no change in his basic ideas; rather they represent a further
elaboration of them in certain specific contexts.

Nor was the establishment of Jewish cultural institutions on a
wide scale a repudiation of his earlier views on assimilation. On the
contrary he had always stressed the fact that the path to voluntary
amalgamation lay only through the fullest achievement of national
rights in all their aspects.

To be sure, the present historical period has witnessed a great national upsurge, as the Soviet writer Alexander Sobolev states in these words:

> Ours is an epoch of the growth, self-assertion and rapid development of nations, of the growth of national cultures, national awareness and national pride. Influenced by the ideas and power of socialism, this process is historically of world-wide significance, for it is changing the character of humanity. The development of nations will continue in the foreseeable future, fostering as it does national patriotic consciousness. (*To Strengthen the Unity of the Communist Movement,* Novosti Press Agency Publishing House, Moscow, 1973.

But it would be wrong to conclude from this that the historical trend is now toward growing national distinctness, not toward amalgamation. The process which Sobolev describes is in the main the fruit of the victories of the national liberation struggles, especially in Africa. However, these very victories are creating the conditions, which Lenin noted, for the voluntary coming together of nations and nationalities. More, national development entails the building of a modern industrial economy, which colonialism had held back, and which leads to growing economic interdependence and cultural intercourse. This is already reflected, for example, in the formation of the Organization of African Unity.

In short, the basic tendency remains that defined by Lenin even before World War I. Certainly, nothing has happened to reverse the process of assimilation of national minorities such as in the Soviet Jews.

* * *

Lenin wrote little on the subject of Zionism, though it is clear, as we have noted, that he was totally opposed to it as a most reactionary manifestation of bourgeois nationalism. Recognizing the class roots of anti-Semitism, he proposed to combat it by fighting all forms of discrimination against Jews. And he saw its solution in the abolition of its class roots—in the victory of socialism. This approach has always been rejected by Zionism, which has contended that socialism not only is incapable of doing away with anti-Semitism but in fact promotes it.

Anti-Semitism, it is asserted by contemporary Zionist spokesmen, is historically a feature of the socialist movement. Thus,

Marie Syrkin, a leading figure in the U.S. Zionist movement, maintains "that the non-Jewish radicals have often proven to be openly anti-Semitic and that Communist movements, as in Eastern Europe, have spewed out their zealous Jewish disciples." She speaks of "the socialist doctrinaire hostility to Jews, be it Marx's notorious essay on the Jewish question, in which he states that the essence of Judaism is the profit motive, or Proudhon's view that the Jews are the spirit of finance, or the statements of such German Social Democrats as Franz Mehring or Wilhelm Liebknecht." She adds other examples: the Austrian Social-Democratic Party and the anarchist Russian Narodnaya Volya, the latter of which regarded anti-Semitism, even pogroms, as having revolutionary potential. In her view there is an inherent connection between anti-Semitism and the Left. (*Congress Bi-Weekly*, March 30, 1973.)

Similarly, the U.S. sociologist Seymour Martin Lipset asserts that the Left has historically been afflicted by anti-Semitism in various forms. And he adds, apparently in reference to Lenin among others, that where the Left *has* supported Jewish political and social rights, it has assumed that "one of the payments the Jews would make to the Left for having liberated them would be to disappear—i.e., to become assimilated." ("Anti-Semitism of the Old Left and the New Left," *Encounter*, December 1969.)

These and numerous similar allegations, it should be noted, indiscriminately lump together under the term "Left" all sorts of trends and ideologies. The term is even more loosely used in the charge by Zionist sources that today "anti-Semitism of the Left" has grown to monstrous proportions and has become the chief threat to the Jewish people. Here the "Left" ranges from the Soviet Union and the Arab countries to the New Left, major sections of the Black liberation movement and the Communist Party of the United States.

This is, it must be said, a gross slander. Communists in particular have been the most resolute fighters against all national and racial discrimination and oppression.

This alleged monster is created by the simple device of equating anti-Zionism with anti-Semitism. Israel's foreign minister Abba Eban makes this plain when he states: "Let there be no mistake: the New Left is the author and the progenitor of the new anti-Semitism. One of the chief tasks of any dialogue with the Gentile world is to prove that the distinction between anti-Semitism and anti-Zionism is no distinction at all. Anti-Zionism is merely the new anti-Semitism." (*Congress Bi-Weekly,* March 30, 1973.)

At the heart of this "anti-Semitism of the Left" lies the spurious charge that the Soviet government follows an official policy of anti-Semitism, of cultural genocide for Soviet Jews, compounded by wholesale refusal of their right to migrate to Israel where they may "live as Jews." They are, it is alleged, being forcibly assimilated, being made "to disappear as Jews." Lenin was wrong, we are told; it is widely charged that the Soviet Union is guilty of brutal persecution of Jews, some of its accusers going so far as to compare it with Nazi Germany.

These slanderous allegations, it can readily be shown, have no basis in fact but are malicious concoctions of Right-wing reaction in concert with Zionism aimed at undermining the Soviet Union and promoting the migration of Soviet Jews to Israel. We cannot undertake to expose these falsehoods here; this has been done elsewhere.*

Here we would only note that "anti-Semitism of the Left" and "Soviet anti-Semitism" are simply frauds designed to conceal the fact that socialism does indeed provide a solution to the Jewish question as it does to the national question generally—in fact, the only real solution. From a wretched, degraded, poverty-ridden ghetto existence Soviet Jews have risen to the status of Soviet citizens on a par with all others. This is truly a remarkable achievement, a tribute to the correctness of Lenin's views and actions on the Jewish question.

New York City, January, 1974   Hyman Lumer

* See, for example, the writer's book *Zionism: Its Role in World Affairs,* International Publishers, New York, 1973.

DOES THE JEWISH PROLETARIAT NEED
AN "INDEPENDENT POLITICAL PARTY"?

No. 105 of *Posledniye Izvestia*[1] (January 28/15, 1903), published by the Foreign Committee of the General Jewish Workers' Union of Lithuania, Poland, and Russia, carries a brief article entitled "Concerning a Certain Manifesto" (viz., the manifesto issued by the Ekaterinoslav Committee of the Russian Social-Democratic Labor Party) containing the following statement, which is as extraordinary as it is significant and indeed "fraught with consequences": "The Jewish proletariat has formed itself (*sic!*) into an independent (*sic!*) political party, the Bund."

We did not know this before. This is something new.

Hitherto the Bund[2] has been a constituent part of the Russian Social-Democratic Labor Party, and in No. 106 of *Posledniye Izvestia* we still (still!) find a statement of the Central Committee of the Bund, bearing the heading "Russian Social-Democratic Labor Party." It is true that at its latest congress, the Fourth, the Bund decided to change its name (without stipulating that it would like to hear the Russian comrades' opinion on the name a section of the Russian Social-Democratic Labor Party should bear) and to "introduce" new *federal* relations into the Rules of the Russian Party. The Bund's Foreign Committee has even "introduced" these relations, if that word can be used to describe the fact that it has withdrawn from the Union of Russian Social-Democrats Abroad and has concluded a federal agreement with the latter.

On the other hand, when *Iskra* polemized with the decisions of the Bund's Fourth Congress, the Bund itself stated very definitely that it only wanted to *secure the acceptance of its wishes* and *decisions* by the R.S.D.L.P.; in other words, it flatly and categorically acknowledged that until the R.S.D.L.P. adopted new Rules and settled new forms of its attitude towards the Bund, the latter would remain a section of the R.S.D.L.P.

But now, suddenly, we are told that the Jewish proletariat has already *formed itself* into an *independent* political party! We repeat—this is something new.

Equally new is the furious and foolish onslaught of the Bund's Foreign Committee upon the Ekaterinoslav Committee. We have at last (*though unfortunately after much delay*) received a copy of this manifesto, and we do not hesitate to say that in attacking a manifesto *like this* the Bund has *undoubtedly taken a serious political step.** This step fully accords with the Bund's proclamation as an independent political party and throws much light on the physiognomy and behavior of this new party.

We regret that lack of space prevents us from reprinting the Ekaterinoslav manifesto in full (it would take up about two columns in *Iskra***), and shall confine ourselves to remarking that this admirable manifesto excellently explains to the Jewish workers of the *city of Ekaterinoslav* (we shall presently explain why we have emphasized these words) the Social-Democratic attitude towards Zionism and anti-Semitism. Moreover, the manifesto treats the sentiments, moods, and desires of the Jewish workers so considerately, with such comradely consideration, that it specially refers to and emphasizes the necessity of fighting under the banner of the R.S.D.L.P. *"even for the preservation and further development of your* [the manifesto addresses the Jewish workers] *national culture," "even from the standpoint of purely national interests"* (underlined and italicized in the manifesto itself).

Nevertheless, the Bund's Foreign Committee (we almost said the new party's Central Committee) has fallen upon the manifesto for *making no mention of the Bund.* That is the manifesto's only crime, but one that is terrible and unpardonable. It is for this that the Ekaterinoslav Committee is accused of lacking in "political sense." The Ekaterinoslav comrades are chastised for not "yet having digested the idea of the necessity for a separate organisation [a profound and significant idea!] of the forces [!!] of the Jewish proletariat," for "still harboring the absurd hope of somehow getting rid of it" (the Bund), for spreading the "no less dangerous fable"

---

* That is, of course, if the Bund's Foreign Committee expresses the views of the Bund as a whole on this question.

** We intend to reprint in full the manifesto and the attack of the Bund's Foreign Committee in a pamphlet which we are preparing for the press.

(no less dangerous than the Zionist fable) that anti-Semitism is connected with the bourgeois strata and with their interests, and not with those of the working class. That is why the Ekaterinoslav Committee is advised to "abandon the harmful habit of keeping silent about the independent Jewish working-class movement" and to "reconcile itself to the fact that the Bund exists."

Now, let us consider whether the Ekaterinoslav Committee is actually guilty of a crime, and whether it really should have mentioned the Bund without fail. Both questions can be answered only in the negative, for the simple reason that the manifesto is not addressed to the "Jewish workers" in general (as the Bund's Foreign Committee quite wrongly stated), but to "the Jewish workers *of the city of Ekaterinoslav*" (the Bund's Foreign Committee forgot to quote these last words!). *The Bund has no organization* in Ekaterinoslav. (And, in general, regarding the south of Russia the Fourth Congress of the Bund passed a resolution *not to organize separate committees of the Bund* in cities where the Jewish organizations are included in the Party committees and where their needs can be fully satisfied without separation from the committees.) Since the Jewish workers in Ekaterinoslav are not organized in a separate committee, it follows that their movement (inseparably from the entire working-class movement in that area) is wholly guided by the Ekaterinoslav Committee, which subordinates them *directly* to the R.S.D.L.P., which *must* call upon them to work *for the whole Party*, and not for its individual sections. It is clear that under these circumstances the Ekaterinoslav Committee was not obliged to mention the Bund; on the contrary, if it had presumed to advocate "the necessity for a separate organization of the forces [it would rather and more probably have been an organization of *impotence**] of the Jewish proletariat" (which is what the Bundists want), it would have made a very

---

* It is this task of "organizing impotence" that the Bund serves when, for example, it uses such a phrase as "our comrades of the 'Christian' working-class organizations.'" The phrase is as preposterous as is the whole attack on the Ekaterinoslav Committee. We have no knowledge of any "Christian" working-class organizations. Organizations belonging to the R.S.D.L.P. have never distinguished their members according to religion, never asked them about their religion and never *will*–even when the Bund will *in actual fact* "have formed itself into an independent political party."

grave error and committed a direct breach, not only of the Party
Rules, but of the unity of the proletarian class struggle.

Further, the Ekaterinoslav Committee is accused of lack of
"orientation" in the question of anti-Semitism. The Bund's Foreign
Committee betrays truly infantile views on important social
movements. The Ekaterinoslav Committee speaks of the
international anti-Semitic movement of the *last decades* and remarks that "from Germany this movement spread to other countries and everywhere found adherents among the bourgeois, and
not among the working-class sections of the population." "This is a
no less dangerous fable" (than the Zionist fables), cries the
thoroughly aroused Bund's Foreign Committee. Anti-Semitism
"has struck roots in the mass of the workers," and to prove this the
"well-oriented" Bund cites two facts: 1) workers' participation in a
pogrom in Czestochowa and 2) the behaviour of 12 (*twelve*!) Christian workers in Zhitomir, who scabbed on the strikers and
threatened to "kill off all the Yids." Very weighty proofs indeed,
especially the latter! The editors of *Posledniye Izvestia* are so ac-
customed to dealing with big strikes involving five or ten workers
that the behavior of twelve ignorant Zhitomir workers is dragged
out as evidence of the link between international anti-Semitism
and one "section" or another "of the population." This is, indeed,
magnificent! If, instead of flying into a foolish and comical rage at
the Ekaterinoslav Committee, the Bundists had pondered a bit
over this question and had consulted, let us say, Kautsky's pamphlet on the social revolution,[3] a Yiddish edition of which they
themselves published recently, they would have understood the
link that *undoubtedly* exists between anti-Semitism and the interests of the bourgeois, and not of the working-class sections of
the population. If they had given it a little more thought they
might have realized that the social character of anti-Semitism today
is not changed by the fact that dozens or even hundreds of unor-
ganized workers, nine-tenths of whom are still quite ignorant, take
part in a pogrom.

The Ekaterinoslav Committee has risen up (and rightly so)
against the Zionist fable about anti-Semitism being eternal; by
making its angry comment the Bund had only confused the issue
and planted in the minds of the Jewish workers ideas which tend to
blunt their class-consciousness.

From the viewpoint of the struggle for political liberty and for socialism being waged by the whole working class of Russia, the Bund's attack on the Ekaterinoslav Committee is the height of folly. From the viewpoint of the Bund as "an independent political party," this attack becomes understandable: don't dare anywhere organize "Jewish" workers together with, and inseparably from, "Christian" workers! If you would address the Jewish workers in the name of the Russian Social-Democratic Labor Party or its committees, don't dare do so directly, over our heads, ignoring the Bund or making no mention of it!

And this profoundly regrettable fact is not accidental. Having once demanded "federation" instead of autonomy in matters concerning the Jewish proletariat, you were *compelled* to proclaim the Bund an "independent political party" in order to carry out this principle of federation *at all costs*. However, your declaring the Bund an independent political party is just that reduction to an absurdity of your fundamental error in the national question which will inescapably and inevitably be the starting-point of a change in the views of the Jewish proletariat and of the Jewish Social-Democrats in general. "Autonomy" under the Rules adopted in 1898 provides the Jewish working-class movement with all it needs: propaganda and agitation in Yiddish, its own literature and congresses, the right to advance separate demands to supplement a single general Social-Democratic program and to satisfy local needs and requirements arising out of the special features of Jewish life. In everything else there must be complete fusion with the Russian proletariat, in the interests of the struggle waged by the entire proletariat of Russia. As for the fear of being "steam-rollered" on the event of such fusion, the very nature of the case makes it groundless, since it is autonomy that is a guarantee against all "steam-rolling" in matters pertaining specifically to the *Jewish* movement, while in matters pertaining to the struggle against the autocracy, the struggle against the bourgeoisie of Russia as a whole, we must act as a single and centralized militant organization, have behind us the whole of the proletariat, without distinction of language or nationality, a proletariat whose unity is cemented by the continued joint solution of problems of theory and practice, of tactics and organization; and we must not set up organizations that would march separately, each along its own track; we must not weaken the force of our offensive by breaking up into numerous independent political parties; we must not introduce estrangement and isolation and then have to heal an artificially implanted disease with the aid of these notorious "federation" plasters.

Iskra, No. 34
February 15, 1903

Published according
to the *Iskra* text

SECOND CONGRESS OF THE R.S.D.L.P.
(July 17 (30)—August 10 (23), 1903 (Excerpts)

DRAFT RESOLUTION ON THE PLACE OF THE BUND IN THE PARTY

Taking into consideration that the fullest and closest unity of the
militant proletariat is absolutely essential both for the purpose of
the earliest achievement of its ultimate aim and in the interests of
an unswerving political and economic struggle in conditions of the
existing society;

that, in particular, complete unity between the Jewish and non-
Jewish proletariat is moreover especially necessary for a successful
struggle against anti-Semitism, this despicable attempt of the government and the exploiting classes to exacerbate racial particularism and national enmity;

that the complete amalgamation of the Social-Democratic organizations of the Jewish and non-Jewish proletariat can in no respect or manner restrict the independence of our Jewish comrades
in conducting propaganda and agitation in one language or
another, in publishing literature adapted to the needs of a given
local or national movement, or in advancing such slogans for agitation and the direct political struggle that would be an application
and development of the general program regarding full equality
and full freedom of language, national culture, etc., etc.;

the Congress emphatically repudiates federation as the organizational principle of a Russian party and endorses the organizational
principle adopted as the basis of the Rules of 1898, i.e., autonomy
for the national Social-Democratic organizations in matters concerning. . . . [Here the manuscript breaks off.—*Ed.*]

Written in June-July, 1903   Published according
First published in 1927   to the manuscript
in *Lenin Miscellany VI*

WITHDRAWAL OF THE BUND (DRAFT RESOLUTION NOT SUBMITTED TO THE CONGRESS)

The Congress considers the refusal of the Bund delegates to submit to the decision adopted by the majority of the Congress as the Bund's withdrawal from the R.S.D.L.P.

The Congress deeply regrets this step, which, it is convinced, is a major political mistake . . .* on the part of the leaders of the "Jewish Workers' Union," a mistake which must inevitably injure the interests of the Jewish proletariat and working-class movement. The Congress considers that the arguments cited by the Bund delegates in justification of their step amount in practice to entirely unfounded apprehensions and suspicion that the Social-Democratic convictions of the Russian Social-Democrats are insincere and inconsistent; in respect of theory they are the result of the unfortunate penetration of nationalism into the Social-Democratic movement of the Bund.

The Congress voices its desire for, and firm conviction of, the need for complete and closest unity of the Jewish and Russian working-class movement in Russia, unity not only in principle by also in organization, and resolves to take all measures in order to acquaint the Jewish proletariat in detail both with this resolution of the Congress and with the general attitude of the Russian Social-Democrats towards every national movement.

Written on August 5 (18)—10 (23), 1903
First published in 1930
in *Lenin Miscellany* XV

Published according
to the manuscript

SPEECH ON THE PLACE OF THE BUND IN THE R.S.D.L.P. JULY 20 (AUGUST 2)

I shall first deal with Hofman's[4] speech and his expression "a compact majority." Comrade Hofman uses these words by way of reproach. In my opinion we should be proud, not ashamed, of the

---

* One word here is indecipherable.—Ed.

fact that there is a compact majority at the Congress. And we shall be prouder still if our whole Party proves to be a compact, a highly compact, 90 per cent, majority. (*Applause*.) The majority were right in making the position of the Bund in the Party the first item on the agenda and the Bundists at once proved this by submitting their so-called Rules, but in essence proposing *federation*. Once there are members in the Party who propose federation and others who reject it, there could be no other course open but to make the question of the Bund the first item on the agenda. It is no use forcing your favors on anybody, and the internal affairs of the Party cannot be discussed until we have firmly and uncompromisingly settled whether or not we want to march together.

The crux of the issue has not always been presented quite correctly in the debate. The point of the matter is that, in the opinion of many Party members, federation is *harmful* and runs counter to the principles of Social-Democracy as applied to existing Russian conditions. Federation is harmful because it *sanctions* segregation and alienation, elevates them to a principle, to a law. Complete alienation does indeed prevail among us, and we ought not to sanction it, or cover it with a fig-leaf, but combat it and resolutely acknowledge and proclaim the necessity of firmly and unswervingly advancing towards the *closest* unity. That is why we reject federation in principle, *in limine** (as the Latin phrase has it); that is why we reject *all* obligatory partitions that serve to divide us. As it is, there will always be different groupings in the Party, groupings of comrades, tactics or organization; but let there be only *one* division into groups throughout the Party, that is, let all like-minded members join in a single group, instead of groups first being formed in *one section* of the Party, separately from the groups in another section of the Party, and then having a union not of groups holding different views or different shades of opinion, but of sections of the Party, each containing different groups. I repeat, we recognize no *obligatory* partitions, and that is why we reject federation in principle.

I shall now pass to the question of autonomy. Comrade Lieber has said that federation means centralism, while autonomy means decentralism. Can it be that Comrade Lieber takes the Congress

---

* On the threshold.—*Ed.*

members for six-year-old children, who may be regaled with such sophistries? Is it not clear that centralism demands the *absence* of all partitions between the central body and even the most remote and out-of-the-way sections of the Party? Our central body will be given the absolute right to communicate directly with every Party member. The Bundists would only laugh if someone would propose to them a form of "centralism" *within* the Bund, under which its Central Committee could not communicate with all the Kovno groups and comrades otherwise than through the Kovno Committee. Incidentally, as regards the committees: Comrade Lieber has exclaimed with feeling, "What is the good of talking about the Bund's autonomy if it is to be an organization subordinated to one central body? After all, you would not grant autonomy to some Tula Committee!" You are mistaken, Comrade Lieber; we will certainly and most decidedly grant autonomy to "some" Tula Committee, too, autonomy in the sense of freedom from petty interference by the central body, although the duty of obeying that body will, of course, remain. I have taken the words "petty interference" from the Bund leaflet, "Autonomy or Federation?" The Bund has advanced this freedom from "petty interference" as a *condition*, as a *demand* to the Party. The mere fact that it advances such ridiculous demands shows how muddled the Bund is on the question at issue. Does the Bund really think that the Party would tolerate the existence of a central body that indulged in "*petty*" interference in the affairs of *any* Party organization or group? Is this not, in effect, precisely that "organized distrust" which has already been mentioned at this Congress? Such distrust runs through all the proposals and arguments of the Bundists. Is it not, in fact, the *duty* of our entire Party to fight, for example, for *full* equality and even for *recognition* of the right of nations to self-determination? Consequently, if any section of our Party failed in this duty, it would unquestionably be liable to condemnation by virtue of our principles; it would unquestionably be liable to *correction* on the part of the central institutions of the Party. And if the neglect of that duty were conscious and deliberate, despite full opportunity to carry out that duty, then that would be *treachery*.

Further, Comrade Lieber has asked us in moving tones *how it can be proved* that autonomy is able to guarantee to the Jewish workers' movement that independence which is absolutely essential to it. A strange question, indeed! How can it be proved that one of the several paths suggested is the right one? The only way is to try it and see. My reply to Comrade Lieber's question is: *March with us*, and we undertake to prove to you in practice that all legitimate demands for independence are gratified in full.

When I hear disputes about the place of the Bund, I always recollect the British miners. They are excellently organized, better than any other workers. And *because of that* they want to thwart the general demand for an 8-hour day put forward by all proletarians.[5] These miners have the same narrow idea of the unity of the proletariat as our Bundists. Let the sad example of the miners serve as a warning to our comrades of the Bund.

First published in
Geneva in 1904 in
the *Minutes of the
Second Regular Congress
of the R.S.D.L.P.*

Published according to
the text of the *Minutes*
and the manuscripts

THE LATEST WORD
IN BUNDIST NATIONALISM

The Foreign Committee of the Bund has just issued a bulletin containing a report on the Fifth Congress of the Bund, which took place in June (Old Style). Preponderant among its resolutions are the "draft Rules" on the position of the Bund in the Party. This draft is highly instructive, and from the angle of definiteness and "resoluteness" of content, nothing better could be desired. Strictly speaking, the first paragraph of the draft is so striking as to reduce all the others to mere explanation or even to entirely useless ballast. "The Bund," declares § 1, "is a *federative* [italics ours] section of the Russian Social-Democratic Labor Party." Federation presupposes an *agreement* between separate, entirely independent units, which define their mutual relations only by voluntary consent of the sides concerned. It is not surprising, therefore, that the "draft Rules" speak repeatedly of the *"contracting parties"* (§§ 3, 8, 12). It is not surprising that, on the basis of this draft, the *Party Congress* is not given the right to alter, supplement or delete *Rules* relating to a *section* of the Party. Neither is it surprising that the Bund reserves to itself "representation" in the Central Committee of the Party and permits this Central Committee of the Party to address itself to the Jewish proletariat and to comminicate with individual sections of the Bund *"only with the consent of the Central Committee of the Bund."* All this logically stems from the concept of "federation," from the concept of "contracting parties,"and had the Fifth Congress of the Bund simply resolved that the Bund is to be constituted as an independent Social-Democratic national (or, perhaps, nationalist Social-Democratic?) party, it would have saved itself (and others) much time, much labor, and much paper. On the one hand, it would have been clear at once without any circumlocution that an independent, separate party could determine its relations with other parties only as a "contracting party"

and only on the basis of "mutual consent." There would have been
no need to enumerate every individual case when such consent
will be required (and it is impossible in fact to enumerate *all* such
cases, while to give an incomplete list, as the Bund does, is to
open the door to a host of misunderstandings). There would have
been no need to do violence to logic and conscience by calling an
agreement between two independent units Rules on the position of
one section of the party. This apparently seemly and suitable name
("Rules on the Position of the Bund in the Party") is all the more
false in essence since the entire Party has in fact not yet restored
its full organizational unity, while the Bund comes out as an already unified section, which wishes to take advantage of the short-
comings in the general organization in order to get still farther
away from the whole, *in order to try and split up this whole into
small parts for all time.*

On the other hand, a straightforward treatment of the matter
would have relieved the authors of the notorious draft Rules of the
necessity to introduce clauses providing for rights already posses-
sed by *every* organized section of the Party, every district organization, every committee and every group, e.g., the right to solve, in
accordance with the Party program, general problems on which
Party congresses have not adopted decisions. To write Rules including clauses such as these is simply ridiculous.

Let us now appraise in essence the stand taken by the Bund.
Once it has stepped on to the inclined plane of nationalism, the
Bund (if it did not wish to renounce its basic mistake) was naturally
and inevitably bound to arrive at the formation of a particular
Jewish party. And this is precisely the direct object of § 2 of the
Rules, which grants the Bund the *monopoly* of representing the
Jewish proletariat. According to this paragraph, the Bund is in the
Party as its (the Jewish proletariat's) *sole* (italics ours) representative. The activities of the Bund and the organization of the Bund
are not to be restricted by any territorial limits. Consequently,
complete separation and demarcation of the Jewish and non-Jewish
proletariat of Russia is not only here effected *to the end* with absolute consistency, but is endorsed by what may be called a notarial
agreement, by "Rules," by a "basic" law (see § 12 of the draft).
Such "outrageous" facts as the audacious appeal of the Ekaterinoslav Committee of the Party to the Jewish workers directly, not

through the medium of the Bund (which had no special organization in Ekaterinoslav at the time!), should henceforth become impossible, according to the idea of the new draft. However few the
number of Jewish workers may be in a given locality, however far
away this locality may be from the centers of the Bundist organization, no section of the Party, not even the Central Committee of
the Party, dare address itself to the Jewish proletariat without the
consent of the Central Committee of the Bund! It is hard to believe that such a proposal could have been made, so monstrous is
this demand for monopoly, especially in our Russian conditions,
but §§ 2 and 8 (footnote) of the draft Rules leave no doubts whatever on this score. The desire of the Bund to shift still farther away
from the Russian comrades is apparent not only in each clause of
the draft, but is also expressed in other resolutions of the congress.
For example, the Fifth Congress has resolved to publish once a
month *Posledniye Izvestia,* issued by the Foreign Committee of
the Bund, "in the form of a newspaper which would explain the
programmatic and tactical position of the Bund." We shall be look-
ing forward with impatience and interest to an explanation of this
position. The congress has *annulled* the resolution of the Fourth
Congress on work in the South. It is known that the Fourth Congress of the Bund decided that *"separate committees of the Bund
shall not be set up"* (italicized by the Bund) in the towns and cities
in the South, where the Jewish organizations are included in the
Party committees. The reversal of this decision is a big step towards further isolation, a direct challenge to the comrades from the
South, who have been working and wanted to work among the
Jewish proletariat, while remaining inseparably connected with the
local proletariat *as a whole.* "He who says A must say B"; one who
has adopted the standpoint of nationalism naturally arrives at the
desire to erect a Chinese Wall around his nationality, his national
working-class movement; he is unembarrassed even by the fact
that it would mean building separate walls in each city, in each
little town and village, unembarrassed even by the fact that by his
tactics of division and dismemberment *he is reducing to nil* the
great call for the rallying and unity of the proletarians of all nations, all races and all languages. And what bitter mockery sounds
in the resolution of the same Fifth Congress of the Bund on pogroms, which expresses the "confidence that *only the joint struggle*

of the proletarians of all nationalities will abolish the conditions giving rise to events similar to those at Kishinev"[6] (italics ours). How false these words about joint struggle sound when we are treated at the very same time to "Rules" which not only keep the joint fighters *far apart*, but strengthen this separation and alienation through organizational means! I should like very much to give the Bund nationalists a piece of advice: learn from those Odessa workers who went on a joint strike and attended joint meetings and joint demonstrations, without first asking (ah, the audacity!) for the "consent" of the Central Committee of the Bund for an appeal to the Jewish nation, and who reassured the shopkeepers with the words (see *Iskra*, No. 45): "Have no fear, have no fear, this is not Kishinev for you, what we want is something else, we have neither Jews nor Russians in our midst, we are *all workers*, life is equally hard for us all." Let the comrades of the Bund ponder over these words, if it is not too late; let them think well about whither they are going!

Iskra, No. 46,   Published according
August 15, 1903   to the *Iskra* text

MAXIMUM BRAZENNESS
AND MINIMUM LOGIC

In our 46th issue we reprinted the resolution of the Fifth Congress of the Bund on the position of the Bund in the R.S.D.L.P., and gave our opinion of it. The Foreign Committee of the Bund replies at great length and with great heat in its leaflet of September 9 (22). The most material part of this angry reply is the following phenomenal revelation: *"In addition to its maximum Rules [sic!], the Fifth Congress of the Bund also drew up minimum Rules"*; and these minimum Rules are quoted in full, it being explained in two notes, moreover, that "the rejection of autonomy" and the demand that other sections of the Party appeal to the Jewish proletariat only with the sanction of the Bund Central Committee *"must be put forward as an ultimatum."* Thus decided the Fifth Congress of the Bund.

Charming, is it not? The Bund Congress draws up two sets of Rules *simultaneously*, defining simultaneously both its maximum and minimum desires or demands. The minimum it prudently (oh, so prudently!) tucks away in its pocket. Only the maximum is published (in the leaflet of August 7 [20]), and it is *publicly* announced, clearly and explicitly, that this maximum draft is "to be submitted to the Second Congress of the Russian Social-Democratic Labor Party as the *basis* for the discussion [mark that!] of the Bund's position in the Party." The Bund's opponents, naturally, attack this maximum with the utmost vehemence, just because it is the maximum, the "last word"* of the trend they condemn. Thereupon, *a*

---

* By the way, it is extremely characteristic of the Bund's methods of controversy that this expression called down on our heads the particular wrath of *Posledniye Izvestia*. Why the last word, it demanded, when it (the demand for federation) had been uttered over two years ago? *Iskra* was counting on the short memory of its readers! . . . Calm yourselves, calm yourselves, gentlemen! The author of the article called your maximum Rules the last word because *that word* was uttered two days (approximately) before No. 46 of *Iskra*, and not two years ago.

month later, these people, without the slightest embarrassement, pull the "minimum" out of their pocket, and add the ominous word: *"ultimatum"*!

That is a positive *last price,* not a "last word" . . . Only is it really your last, gentlemen? Perhaps you've got a minimal minimum in another pocket? Perhaps in another month or so we shall be seeing that?

We very much fear that the Bundists do not quite realize all the "beauty" of this maximum and minimum. Why, how else can you haggle than by asking an exorbitant price, then knocking off 75 per cent and declaring, "That's my last price"? Why, is there any difference between haggling and politics?

There is, gentlemen, we make bold to assure you. Firstly, in politics some parties adhere systematically to certain *principles,* and it is indecent to haggle over principles. Secondly, when people who claim to belong to a party regard certain of their demands as an ultimatum, that is, as the very condition of their membership in the party, political honesty requires that they should not conceal the fact, should not tuck it away *"for the time being"* in their pocket, but, on the contrary, should say so openly and definitely right from the start.

We have been preaching these simple truths to the Bundists for a long time. As early as February (in our 33rd issue) we wrote that it was stupid and unbefitting to play hide-and-seek, and that the Bund had acted separately (in issuing its statement about the Organizing Committee) because it wanted to act *as a contracting party* and present terms to the Party as a whole.* For this opinion we were drenched with a whole bucketful of specifically Bundist (one might with equal justice say, specifically fish-market) abuse, yet *events have now shown that we were right.* It is indeed as a *contracting party* that the Bund comes forward in the decisions of its Fifth Congress, presenting outright ultimatums to the Party as a whole! That is just what we have been trying all along to get the Bundists to admit, by showing that it followed inevitably from the position they had taken up; they angrily protested, dodged and wriggled, but in the end were obliged after all to produce their "minimum."

* *See Collected Works,* Vol. 6, pp. 319-25.—*Ed.*

That is funny; but funnier still is the fact that the Bund continues to wriggle even now, continues to talk about the "falsity" of "*Iskra's*" old, generally known fabrication to the effect that the Bund wants to form a federal alliance with the Russian Party." That is a lying fabrication, it claims, because Paragraph 1 of the Rules proposed by the Bund distinctly speaks of its desire to be a component element of the Party, not to form an alliance with it.

Very good, gentlemen! But does not this same paragraph say that the Bund is a *federated* component of the Party? Don't your maximum Rules refer throughout to contracting parties? Don't the minimum Rules speak of an *ultimatum,* and make any change in their "fundamental clauses" contingent on the mutual consent of the component elements of the Party, neither the local nor the district organizations, moreover, being recognized as such for this purpose? You yourselves say that neither local nor district organizations, but only "integral elements of the same nature as the Bund" can be contracting parties. You yourselves mention by way of example that "the Polish, Lithuanian or Lettish Social-Democrats" might be regarded as such integral elements, "*if they belonged to the Party,*" as you sensibly add. But what if they do not belong to the Party? And what if the federation of national organizations which you find desirable is found undesirable and emphatically rejected by all the rest of the Party? You know very well that that is how matters stand; you yourselves expressly say you no longer demand that the whole Party be built on the basis of a federation of nationalities. *To whom,* then, are you addressing your *ultimatum*? Is it not obvious that you are addressing it to the whole Party, minus the Bund? Instead of convicting *Iskra* of a lying fabrication, you only convict yourselves of a minimum of logic in your subterfuges.

But look, the Bundists protest, in our minimum Rules we have even deleted the federation demand! This deletion of the "dreadful" word is indeed the most interesting episode in the famous transition from maximum to minimum. Nowhere else, perhaps, has the Bund's unconcern for principles betrayed itself so naively. You are dogmatists, hopeless dogmatists, we are told; nothing in the world will induce you to recognize the federal "principle of organization." We, on the other hand, are not dogmatists, we "put the matter on a purely practical footing." Is it some principle you don't like? Queer fellows! Why, then we'll do without any principle at all, we'll "formulate Paragraph 1 in such a way that it shall not be a declaration of a definite principle of organization." "The crux of the matter does not lie in the statement of principle prefacing the Rules, but in the concrete clauses, which are derived from an examination of the needs of the Jewish working-class movement, on the one hand, and of the movement as a whole, on the other" (leaflet of September 9 [22], p. 1).

The naïvete of this argument is so delightful that one just wants to hug the author. The Bundist seriously believes that it is only certain dreadful words the dogmatists fear, and so he decides that if these words are deleted, the dogmatist will see nothing objectionable in the concrete clauses themselves! And so he toils in the sweat of his brow, draws up his maximum Rules, gets in reserve his minimum Rules (against a rainy day), draws up ultimatum No. 1, ultimatum No. 2. . . . *Oleum et operam perdidisti, amice!*—you are wasting time and effort, my friend. Inspite of the cunning (oh, wonderfully cunning!) removal of the label, the dogmatist detects the federal principle in the minimum's "concrete clauses" too. That principle is to be seen in the demand that a component element of the Party should not be limited by any territorial bounds, and in the claim to be the "sole"* representative of the Jewish proletariat, and in the demand for "representation" on the Party Central Committee; in the denial to the Party Central Committee of the right to communicate with any part of the Bund without the consent of the Bund Central Committee; in the demand that fundamental clauses should not be changed without the consent of the *component elements* of the Party.

No, gentlemen, the crux of this matter of the Bund's position in the Party does lie in the declaration of a definite principle of organization, and not at all in the concrete clauses. The crux of the matter is a *choice* of ways. Is the historically evolved isolation of the Bund to be legitimized, or is it to be rejected on principle, and the course openly, definitely, firmly and honestly adopted of ever

---

* "This word is of no significance," the Bund now assures us. Strange! Why should a word that has no significance have been inserted in both minimum and maximum? In the Russian language the word has a perfectly definite significance. What it signifies in the present instance is a "declaration" of both federalism and nationalism. We would advise the Bundists, who can see no connection between nationalism and federation, to ponder this point.

closer and closer union and fusion with the Party as a whole? Is this isolation to be preserved, or a *turn made towards fusion*? That is the question.

The answer will depend on the free will of the Bund, for, as we already said in our 33rd issue, "love cannot be forced." If you *want* to move towards fusion, you will reject federation and accept autonomy. You will understand in that case that autonomy guarantees a process of fusion so gradual that the reorganization would proceed with the minimum of dislocation, and in such a way, moreover, that the Jewish working-class movement would lose nothing and gain everything by this reorganization and fusion.

If you do not want to move towards fusion, you will stand for federation (whether in its maximum or minimum form, whether with or without a declaration); you will be afraid of being "steamrollered," you will turn the regrettable isolation of the Bund into a fetish, and will cry that the abolition of this isolation means the destruction of the Bund; you will begin to seek grounds justifying your isolation, and in this search will now grasp at the Zionist idea of a Jewish "*nation,*" now resort to demagogy and scurrilities.

Federalism can be justified theoretically only on the basis of nationalist ideas, and it would be strange if we had to prove to the Bundists that it was no mere accident that the declaration of federalism was made at that very Fourth Congress which proclaimed the Jews to be a nation.

The idea of fusion can be discredited in practice only by inciting politically unenlightened and timid people against the "monstrous," "Arakcheyev"[7] organizational plan of *Iskra,* which supposedly wants to "regiment" the committees and not allow them to "take a single step without orders from above." How terrible! We have no doubt that all the committees will now hasten to revolt against the iron glove, the Arakcheyev fist, etc. . . . But where, gentlemen, did you get your information about this brutal organizational plan? From our literature? Then why not quote it? Or from the tales of idle Party gossips, who can tell you on the very best authority all, absolutely all the details regarding this Arakcheyevism? The latter supposition is probably the more correct, for even people with a minimum of logic could hardly confuse the very necessary demand that the Central Committee should "*be able* to communicate with every Party member"* with the patently scurrilous bugbear that the Central Committee will "do everything itself" and "lay down the law on everything." Or another thing: what is this nonsense that "between the periphery and the center" there will be *"lose Organisationen"?*** We can guess: our worthy Bundists heard something, but did not know what it was all about. We shall have to explain it to them at length on some suitable occasion.

But, worst of all, it is not only the local committees that will have to revolt, but the Central Committee too. True, it has not been born yet,[8] but the gossips know for certain not only the birthday of the infant but its whole subsequent career. It appears it will be a Central Committee *"directed by a group of writers."* Such a tried and cheap method of warfare, this. The Bundists are not the first to employ it and most likely will not be the last. To convict this Central Committee, or the Organizing Committee, of any mistake, you have to find proof. To convict people of not acting as they themselves think necessary, but of being *directed* by others, you must have the courage to bring charges openly and be ready to answer for them to the whole Party! All that is too dear, too dear in every respect. Gossips' tales, on the other hand, are cheap. . . . And perhaps the fish will bite. It is not pleasant, after all, to be considered a man (or institution) who is "directed," who is in leading strings, who is a pawn, a creature, a puppet of *Iskra.* . . . Our poor, poor future Central Committee! Where will it find a protector against the Arakcheyev yoke? Perhaps in the "independently acting" Bundists, those strangers to all "suspiciousness"?

Iskra, No.49,
October 1, 1903
Published according to
the Iskra text

---

* See p. 10—*Ed.*
** Loose, broad organizations.—*Ed.*

THE POSITION
OF THE BUND IN THE PARTY

Under this title the Bund has published a translation of an article from No. 34 of the *Arbeiterstimme*. [9] This article, accompanying the decisions of the Fifth Bund Congress, represents as it were an official commentary on those decisions. It attempts to give a systematic exposition of all the arguments which lead to the conclusion that the Bund "must be a federated component of the Party." It will be interesting to examine these arguments.

The author begins by stating that the most burning question facing the Russian Social-Democratic movement is the question of unity. On what basis can it be effected? The Manifesto of 1898[10] took the principle of autonomy as the basis. The author examines this principle and finds it to be logically false and inherently contradictory. If by questions which specifically concern the Jewish proletariat are meant only such as relate to methods of agitation (with reference to the specific language, mentality and culture of the Jews), that will be technical (?) autonomy. But such autonomy will mean the destruction of all independence, for it is an autonomy enjoyed by every Party committee, and to put the Bund on a par with the committees will be a denial of autonomy. If, on the other hand, autonomy is understood to mean autonomy in some questions of the program, it is unreasonable to deprive the Bund of all independence in the other questions of the program; and independence in questions of program necessarily involves representation of the Bund, as such, on the central bodies of the Party—that is, not autonomy, but federation. A sound basis for the position of the Bund in the Party must be sought in the history of the Jewish revolutionary movement in Russia, and what that history shows is that all organizations active among the Jewish workers joined to form a single union—the Bund—and that its activities spread from Lithuania to Poland and then to the South of Russia.

Consequently, history broke down all regional barriers and brought forward the Bund as the sole representative of the Jewish proletariat. And there you have a principle which is not the fruit of an idle brain (?) but follows from the whole history of the Jewish working-class movement: the Bund is the sole representative of the interests of the Jewish proletariat. And, naturally, the organization of the proletariat of a whole nationality can enter the Party only if the latter has a federal structure: the Jewish proletariat is not only part of the world family of proletarians, but also part of the Jewish nation, which occupies a special position among the nations. Lastly, it is federation that denotes close unity between the component elements of the Party, for its chief feature is direct participation by each of them in Party affairs, and they all feel they have equal rights. Under autonomy, on the other hand, the components of the Party have no rights, and there is indifference to its common affairs, and mutual distrust, friction and conflict.

Such is the author's line of argument, which we have presented almost entirely in his own words. It boils down to three things: considerations of a general nature as to the inherent contradictoriness of autonomy and its unsuitability from the standpoint of close unity between the components of the Party; lessons from history, which has made the Bund the sole representative of the Jewish proletariat; and, lastly, the affirmation that the Jewish proletariat is the proletariat of a whole nationality, a nationality occupying a special position. Thus the author endeavours to build his case on general principles of organization, on the lessons of history, and on the idea of nationality. He tries—we must give him his due—to examine the matter from all angles. And for that very reason his statement of the case brings out so saliently the attitude of the Bund on this question which is of deep concern to all of us.

Under federation, we are told, the components of the Party have equal rights and share directly in its common affairs; under autonomy they have no rights, and as such do not share in the general life of the Party. This argument belongs entirely to the realm of obvious fallacies; it is as like as two peas to those arguments which mathematicians call mathematical sophistries, and which prove— quite logically, at first glance—that twice two are five, that the part is greater than the whole, and so on. There are collections of such mathematical sophistries, and they are of some value to

school children. But it is even embarrassing to have to explain to
people who claim to be the sole representatives of the Jewish proletariat so elementary a sophistry as the attribution of different
meanings to the term "component of the Party" in two parts of one
and the same argument. When they speak of federation, they
mean by a component of the Party a sum-total of organizations in
different localities; but when they speak of autonomy, they mean
by it each local organization separately. Put these supposedly iden-
tical concepts side by side in the same syllogism, and you will arrive inevitably at the conclusion that twice two is five. And if the
Bundists are still unclear as to the nature of their sophistry, let
them consult their own maximum Rules and they will see that it is
under federation that the local organizations communicate with the
Party center *in*directly, and under autonomy—directly. No, our
federalists would do better not to talk about "close unity"! By trying to disprove that federation means the *isolation*, and the autonomy the *fusion* of the different components of the Party, they
only provoke hilarity.

Hardly more successful is the attempt to prove the "logical falsity" of autonomy by dividing the latter into program autonomy
and technical autonomy. The division itself is utterly absurd. Why
should the specific methods of agitation among Jewish workers be
classed under technical questions? What has technique to do with
it, when it is a matter of peculiarities of language, mentality, conditions of life? How can you talk of independence in questions of
program in connection, for example, with the demand for civil
equality for the Jews? The Social-Democratic program only sets
forth the basic demands, common to the entire proletariat, irrespective of occupational, local, national, or racial distinctions. The
effect of these distinctions is that one and the same demand for
complete equality of citizens before the law gives rise to agitation
against one form of inequality in one locality and against another
form of inequality in another locality or in relation to other groups
of the proletariat, and so on. One and the same point in the program will be applied differently depending on differences in conditions of life, differences of culture, differences in the relation of
social forces in different parts of the country, and so forth. Agitation on behalf of one and the same demand in the program will be
carried on in different ways and in different languages taking into

account all these differences. Consequently, autonomy in questions specifically concerning the proletariat of a given race, nation, or district implies that it is left to the discretion of the organization concerned to determine the specific demands to be advanced in pursuance of the common program and the methods of agitation to be employed. The Party as a whole, its central institutions, lay down the common fundamental principles of program and tactics; as to the different methods of carrying out these principles in practice and agitating for them, they are laid down by the various Party organizations subordinate to the center, depending on local, racial, national, cultural, and other differences.

Is there anything unclear about this conception of autonomy? And is it not the sheerest scholasticism to make a division into program autonomy and technical autonomy?

Just see how the concept autonomy is "logically analyzed" in the pamphlet we are examining. "From the total body of questions with which the Social-Democrats have to deal," the pamphlet says in connection with the autonomy principle taken as the basis in the 1898 Manifesto, "there are singled out [sic!!] some questions, which, it is recognized, specifically concern the Jewish proletariat . . . . Where the realm of general questions begins, the autonomy of the Bund ends. . . . This gives rise to a duality in the position of the Bund in the Party: in specific questions it acts as the Bund . . . in general questions it loses its distinctive character and is put on a par with an ordinary committee of the Party. . . ." The Social-Democratic program demands complete equality of all citizens before the law. *In pursuance* of that program the Jewish worker in Vilna puts forward one specific demand, and the Bashkir worker in Ufa an entirely different specific demand. Does that mean that "from the total body of questions" "some are *singled out*"? If the general demand for equality is embodied in a number of specific demands for the abolition of specific forms of inequality, is that a *singling out* of the specific from the general questions? The specific demands are not singled out from the general demands of the program, but are advanced *in pursuance* of them. What is singled out is what specifically concerns the Jew in Vilna as distinct from what specifically concerns the Bashkir in Ufa. The generalization of their demands, the representation of their *common class interests* (and not of their specific occupational, ra-

cial, local, national, or other interests) is the affair of the whole
Party, of the Party center. That would surely seem clear enough!
The reason the Bundists have muddled it is that, instead of logical
analysis, they have again and again given us specimens of logical
fallacies. They have entirely failed to grasp the relation between
the Social-Democrats' general and specific demands. They imagine
that "from the total body of questions with which the Social-
Democrats have to deal, some questions are singled out," when
actually *every* question dealt with in our program is a generalization of a number of specific questions and demands; *every* point in
the program is common to the *entire* proletariat, while at the same
time it is subdivided into specific questions depending on the proletarians' different occupations, their different conditions of life,
differences of language, and so on and so forth. The Bundists are
disturbed by the contradictoriness and duality of the position of the
Bund, consisting, don't you see, in the fact that in specific questions it acts as the Bund, while in general questions it loses its
distinctive character. A little reflection would show them that such
a "duality" exists in the position of *absolutely every*
Social-Democratic worker, who in specific questions acts as a
worker in a particular trade, a member of a particular nation, an
inhabitant of a particular locality, while in general questions he
"loses his distinctive character" and is put on a par with *every other*
Social-Democrat. The autonomy of the Bund, under the Rules of
1898, is of exactly the same nature as the autonomy of the Tula
Committee; only the limits of this autonomy are somewhat different and somewhat wider in the former case than in the latter. And
there is nothing but a crying logical fallacy in the following argument, by which the Bund tries to refute this conclusion: "If the
Bund is allowed independence in some questions of the *program,*
on what grounds is it deprived of *all* independence in the other
questions of the program?" This contrasting of specific and general
questions as "some" and "*the others*" is an inimitable specimen of
Bundist "logical analysis"! These people simply cannot understand
that it is like contrasting the different colors, tastes, and fragrances
of particular apples to the *number* of "other" apples. We make bold
to inform you, gentlemen, that not only some, but every apple has
its special taste, color, and fragrance. Not only in "some" questions
of the program, but *in all without exception,* you are allowed inde-

pendence, gentlemen, but only as far as concerns their application to the specific features of the Jewish proletariat. *Mein teuerer Freund, ich rat' Euch drum zuerst Collegium logicum!**

The second argument of the Bundists is an appeal to history, which is supposed to have brought forward the Bund as the sole representative of the Jewish proletariat.

In the first place, this is not true. The author of the pamphlet himself says that "the work of other organizations [besides the Bund] in this direction [i.e., among the Jewish proletariat] either yielded no results at all, or results too insignificant to merit attention." Hence, on his own admission, there was such work, and consequently the Bund *was not* the *sole* representative of the Jewish proletariat; as regards the results of this work, no one, of course, will rely on the Bund's opinion; and, lastly, it is a known fact that the Bund *interfered* with the work of other organizations among the Jewish proletariat (we have only to mention the well-known incident of its campaign against the Ekaterinoslav Party Committee for daring to issue a proclamation to the Jewish workers[12], so that even if the results did indeed merit no attention, the Bund itself would be partly to blame.

Further, the measure of truth contained in the Bund's historical reference does not in the least prove the soundness of its arguments. The facts which did take place and which the Bund has in mind speak against it, not for it. These facts are that the Bund existed and developed—during the five years since the First Congress—quite separately and independently from the other organizations of the Party. In general, the actual ties between all Party organizations during this period were very weak, but the ties between the Bund and the rest of the Party were not only far weaker than those between the other organizations, but they kept growing weaker all the time. That the Bund itself *weakened* these ties is directly proved by the history of our Party's organizations abroad. In 1898, the Bund members abroad belonged to the one common Party organization; but by 1903 they had left it to form a completely separate and independent organization. The separateness and independence of the Bund is beyond question, as is also the fact that it has steadily become more pronounced.

---

* "Hence, my dear friend, I would advise you to begin with college logic."[11]—*Ed.*

What follows from this unquestionable fact? What follows in the opinion of the Bundists is that one must bow to this fact, slavishly submit to it, turn it into a principle, into the sole principle providing a sound basis for the position of the Bund, and legitimize this principle in the Rules, which should recognize the Bund as the sole representative of the Jewish proletariat in the Party. In our opinion, on the other hand, such a conclusion is the sheerest opportunism, "tail-ism"[13] of the worst kind. The conclusion to be drawn from the five years of disunity is not that this disunity should be legitimized, but that an end should be put to it once and for all. And will anybody still venture to deny that it really was disunity? *All* component parts of the Party developed separately and independently during this period—are we perhaps to deduce from this the "principle" of federation between Siberia, the Caucasus, the Urals, the South, and the rest? The Bundists themselves say that, as regards organizational unity of its components, the Party virtually did not exist—and how can what evolved when the Party did not exist be taken as a pattern for the *restoration* of organizational unity? No, gentlemen, your reference to the history of the disunity that gave rise to isolation proves nothing whatever except that this isolation is abnormal. To deduce a "principle" of *organization* from several years of *disorganization* in the Party is to act like those representatives of the historical school who, as Marx sarcastically observed, were prepared to defend the knout on the grounds that it was historical.

Hence, neither the "logical analysis" of autonomy nor the appeals to history can provide even the shadow of a "principle" justifying the isolation of the Bund. But the Bund's third argument, which invokes the idea of a Jewish nation, is undoubtedly of the nature of a principle. Unfortunately, however, this Zionist idea is absolutely false and essentially reactionary. "The Jews have ceased to be a nation, for a nation without a territory is unthinkable," says one of the most prominent of Marxist theoreticians, Karl Kautsky (see No. 42 of *Iskra* and the separate reprint from it *The Kishinev Massacre and the Jewish Question*, p. 3). And quite recently, examining the problem of nationalities in Austria, the same writer endeavoured to give a scientific definition of the concept nationality and established two principal criteria of nationality: language and territory (*Neue Zeit*,[14] 1903, No. 2). A French Jew, the radical

Alfred Naquet says practically the same thing, word for word, in his controversy with the anti-Semites and the Zionists.[15] "If it pleased Bernard Lazare," he writes of the well-known Zionist, "to consider himself a citizen of a separate nation, that is his affair; but I declare that, although I was born a Jew . . . I do not recognize Jewish nationality. . . . I belong to no other nation but the French. . . . Are the Jews a nation? Although they were one in the remote past, my reply is a categorical *negative*. The concept nation implies certain conditions which do not exist in this case. A nation must have a territory on which to develop, and, in our time at least, until a world confederation has extended this basis, a nation must have a common language. And the Jews no longer have either a territory or a common language. . . . Like myself, Bernard Lazare probably did not know a word of Hebrew, and would have found it no easy matter, if Zionism had achieved its purpose, to make himself understood to his co-racials [*congénères*] from other parts of the world" (*La Petite République*, September 24, 1903). "German and French Jews are quite unlike Polish and Russian Jews. The characteristic features of the Jews include nothing that bears the imprint [*empreinte*] of nationality. If it were permissible to recognize the Jews as a nation, as Drumont does, it would be an artificial nation. The modern Jew is a product of the unnatural selection to which his forebears were subjected for nearly eighteen centuries." All that remains for the Bundists is to develop the theory of a separate Russian-Jewish nation, whose language is Yiddish and their territory the Pale of Settlement.[16]

Absolutely untenable scientifically,* the idea that the Jews form a separate nation is reactionary politically. Irrefutable practical proof of that is furnished by generally known facts of recent history and of present-day political realities. All over Europe, the decline

* Not only national, but even racial peculiarities are denied to the Jews by modern scientific investigators, who give prime prominence to the peculiarities of the *history* of the Jews. "Do the peculiarities of Jewry spring from its racial character?" Karl Kautsky asks, and replies that we do not even know with precision what race means. "There is no need to bring in the concept race, which provides no real answer but only poses new problems. It is enough to trace the history of the Jews to ascertain the reasons for their characteristics." And such an expert in this history as Renan says: "The characteristic features of the Jews and their manner of life are far more a product of social conditions [*nécessités sociales*] by which they have been influenced for centuries than a racial distinction [*phénomène de race*]."[17]

of medievalism and the development of political liberty went hand in hand with the political emancipation of Jews, their abandonment of Yiddish for the language of the people among whom they lived, and, in general, their undeniable progressive assimilation with the surrounding population. Are we again to revert to the exceptionalist theories and proclaim that Russia will be the one exception, although the Jewish emancipation movement is far broader and deeper-rooted here, thanks to the awakening of a heroic class-consciousness among the Jewish proletariat? Can we possibly attribute to chance the fact thast it is the reactionary forces all over Europe, and especially in Russia, who *oppose* the assimilation of the Jews and try to perpetuate their isolation?

That is precisely what the Jewish problem amounts to: assimilation or isolation?—and the idea of a Jewish "nationality" is definitely reactionary not only when expounded by its consistent advocates (the Zionists), but likewise on the lips of those who try to combine it with the ideas of Social-Democracy (the Bundists). The idea of a Jewish nationality runs counter to the interests of the Jewish proletariat, for it fosters among them, directly or indirectly, a spirit hostile to assimilation, the spirit of the "ghetto." When the National Assembly of 1791 decreed the emancipation of the Jews," writes Renan, "it was very little concerned with the question of race. . . . It is the business of the nineteenth century to abolish all 'ghettos,' and I cannot compliment those who seek to restore them. The Jewish race has rendered the world the greatest services. Assimilated with the various nations, harmoniously blended with the various national units, it will render no lesser services in the future than in the past." And Karl Kautsky, in particular reference to the Russian Jews, expresses himself even more vigorously. Hostility towards non-native sections of the population can only be eliminated "when the non-native sections of the population cease to be alien and blend with the general mass of the population. *That is the only possible solution of the Jewish problem, and we should support everything that makes for the ending of Jewish isolation.*" Yet the Bund is resisting this only possible solution, for it is helping, not to end but to increase and legitimize Jewish isolation, by propagating the idea of a Jewish "nation" and a plan of federating Jewish and non-Jewish proletarians. That is the basic mistake of "Bundism," which consistent Jewish Social-Democrats must and

will correct. This mistake drives the Bundists to actions unheard-of
in the international Social-Democratic movement, such as stirring
up distrust among Jewish towards non-Jewish proletarians, foster-
ing suspicion of the latter and disseminating falsehoods about
them. Here is proof, taken from this same pamphlet: "Such an
absurdity [as that the organization of the proletariat of a whole nationality should be denied representation on the central Party
bodies] could be openly advocated only [mark that!] in regard to
the Jewish proletariat, which, owing to the peculiar historical for-
tunes of the Jewish people, still has to fight for equality [!!] in the
world family of the proletariat." We recently came across just such
a trick in a Zionist leaflet, whose authors raved and fumed against
Iskra, purporting to detect in its struggle with the Bund a refusal
to recognize the "equality" of Jew and non-Jew. And now we find
the Bundists repeating the tricks of the Zionists! This is disseminating an outright falsehood, for we have "advocated" "denying representation" not "only" to the Jews, but also also to the Armenians,
the Georgians and so on, and in the case of the Poles, too, we
called for the closest union and fusion of the entire proletariat
fighting against the tsarist-autocracy. It was not for nothing that the
P.S.P. (Polish Socialist Party) raged and fulminated against us! To
call a fight for the Zionist *idea* of a Jewish nation, for the federal
principle of Party organization, a "fight for the equality of the Jews
in the world family of the proletariat" is to degrade the struggle
from the plane of ideas and principles to that of suspicion, incite-
ment and fanning of historically-evolved prejudices. It glaringly
reveals a lack of real ideas and principles as weapons of struggle.

*   *   *

We thus arrive at the conclusion that neither the logical, nor the
historical, nor yet the nationalist arguments of the Bund will stand
criticism. The period of disunity, which aggravated waverings
among the Russian Social-Democrats and the isolation of the various organizations, had the same effect, to an even more marked
degree, in the case of the Bundists. Instead of proclaiming war on
this historically-evolved isolation (further increased by the general
disunity), they elevated it to a principle, seizing for this purpose on
the sophistry that autonomy is inherently contradictory, and on the

Zionist idea of a Jewish nation. Only if it frankly and resolutely admits its mistake and sets out to *move towards fusion* can the Bund turn away from the false path it has taken. And we are convinced that the finest adherents of Social-Democratic ideas among the Jewish proletariat will sooner or later compel the Bund to turn from the path of isolation to that of fusion.

Iskra, No. 51,
October 22, 1903

Published according
to the *Iskra* text

PREFACE TO THE PAMPHLET
MEMORANDUM OF POLICE DEPARTMENT
SUPERINTENDENT LOPUKHIN (Excerpt)

. . . The springs of the police machinery have lost their snap; military force alone is now insufficient. One must stir up national hatred, race hatred; one must recruit "Black Hundreds"[18] from among the politically least developed sections of the urban *(and following that, naturally, the rural)* petty bourgeoisie; one must attempt to rally to the defense of the throne all reactionary elements among the population at large; one must turn the struggle of the police against study circles into a struggle of one part of the people against the other.

That is precisely what the government is now doing when it sets the Tatars against the Armenians in Baku; when it seeks to provoke new pogroms against the Jews; when it organizes Black-Hundred gangs against the Zemstvo people, students, and rebellious Gymnasium youths; and when it appeals to the loyal nobles and to the conservative elements among the peasants. Ah, well! We Social-Democrats are not surprised at these tactics of the autocracy; nor shall we be frightened by them. We know that it will no longer help the government to stir up racial animosity since the workers have begun to organize armed resistance to the pogrom-bandits; and by relying on the exploiting sections of the petty bourgeoisie the government will only antagonize still broader masses of real proletarians. We have never expected any political or social revolutions to come from "convincing" the powers that be, or from educated persons turning to the paths of "virtue." We have always taught that it is the class struggle, the struggle of the exploited part of the people against the exploiters, that lies at the bottom of political transformations and *in the final analysis* determines the fate of all such transformations. By admitting the complete failure of the pettifogging police methods and passing over to the direct organization of civil war, the government shows that *the final reckoning is approaching.* So much the better. It is launching the civil war. So much the better. We, too, are for the civil war. If there is any sphere in which we feel particularly confident, it is here, in the war of the vast masses of the oppressed and the downtrodden, of the toiling millions who keep the whole of society going, against a handful of privileged parasites. Of course, by fanning racial antagonism and tribal hatred, the government may for a time arrest the development of the class struggle, but only for a short time and at the cost of a still greater expansion of the field of the new struggle, at the cost of a more bitter feeling among the people against the autocracy. This is proved by the consequences of the Baku pogrom, which deepened tenfold the revolutionary mood of all sections against tsarism. The government thought to frighten the people by the sight of bloodshed and the vast toll of street battles; but actually it is *dispelling the people's* fear of bloodshed, of a direct armed encounter. Actually, the government is furthering our cause, with agitation of a scope wider and more impressive than we could ever have dreamed of. *Vive le son du canon!* say we in the words of the French revolutionary song: Hail the thunder of the cannon!" Hail the open revolution! Hail the open war of the people against the tsarist government and its adherents!

Written in February-March 1905   Published according to
First published in 1905   the text of the pamphlet
in the pamphlet *Memorandum
of Police Department
Superintendent Lopukhin*
Published by *Vperyod,* Geneva
Signed: *N. LENIN*

TO THE JEWISH WORKERS[19]

In publishing the Report on the Third Congress of the R.S.D.L.P. in Yiddish, the Editorial Board of the Party Central Organ considers it necessary to say a few words in connection with this publication.

The conditions under which the class-conscious proletariat of the whole world lives tend to create the closest bonds and increasing unity in the systematic Social-Democratic struggle of the workers of the various nationalities. The great slogan "Workers of all countries, unite!," which was proclaimed for the first time more than half a century ago, has now become more than the slogan of just the Social-Democratic parties of the different countries. This slogan is being increasingly embodied both among the proletarians of the various nationalities who are struggling under the yoke of one and the same despotic state for freedom and socialism,

In Russia the workers of all nationalities, especially those of non-Russian nationality, endure an economic and political oppression such as obtains in no other country. The Jewish workers, as a disfranchised nationality, not only suffer general economic and political oppression, but they also suffer under the yoke which deprives them of elementary civil rights. The heavier this yoke, the greater the need for the closest possible unity among the proletarians of the different nationalities; for without such unity a victorious struggle against the general oppression is impossible. The more the predatory tsarist autocracy strives to sow the seeds of discord, distrust and enmity among the nationalities it oppresses, the more abominable its policy of inciting the ignorant masses to savage pogroms becomes, the more does the duty devolve upon us, the Social-Democratic Labor Party.

The First Congress of our Party, held in the spring of 1898, set itself the aim of establishing such unity. To dispel any idea of its being national in character, the Party called itself *"Rossiiskaya"* and not *"Russkaya."** The organization of Jewish workers—the Bund—affiliated with the Party as an autonomous section. Unfortunately, from that moment the unity of the Jewish and non-Jewish Social-Democrats within the single party was destroyed. Nationalist ideas began to spread among the leading members of the Bund, ideas which are in sharp contradiction to the entire world view of Social-Democracy. Instead of trying to draw the Jewish and the non-Jewish workers closer together, the Bund embarked upon a policy of weaning the former away from the latter; at its congresses it claimed a separate existence for the Jews as a nation. Instead of carrying on the work begun by the First Congress of the Russian Social-Democratic Party towards still closer unity between the Bund and the Party, the Bund moved a step away from the Party. First, it withdrew from the united organization of the R.S.D.L.P. abroad and set up an independent organization abroad; later, it withdrew from the R.S.D.L.P. as well, when the Second Congress of our Party in 1903 refused by a considerable majority to recognize the Bund as sole representative of the Jewish proletariat. The Bund held to its position, claiming not only that it was the sole representative of the Jewish proletariat, but that no territorial limits were set to its activities. Naturally, the Second Congress of the R.S.D.L.P. could not accept such conditions, since in a number of regions, as, for instance, in South Russia, the organized Jewish proletariat constitutes part of the general Party organization. Ignoring that stand, the Bund withdrew from the Party and thereby broke the unity of the Social-Democratic proletariat, despite the work that had been carried out in common at the Second Congress, and despite the Party Program and Rules.

At its Second and Third Congresses the Russian Social-Democratic Labor Party expressed its firm conviction that the

---

* The adjective *Russkaya* (Russian) pertains to nationality, *Rosiiskaya* (Russian) pertains to Russia as a country.—*Ed.*

Bund's withdrawal from the Party was a grave and deplorable mistake on its part. The Bund's mistake is a result of its basically untenable nationalist views; the result of its groundless claim to be the sole, monopolistic representative of the Jewish proletariat, from which the federalist principle of organization necessarily derives; the result of its long-standing policy of keeping aloof and separate from the Party. We are convinced that this mistake must be rectified and that it will be rectified as the movement continues to grow. We consider ourselves ideologically at one with the Jewish Social-Democratic proletariat. After the Second Congress our Central Committee pursued a non-nationalist policy; it took pains that such committees should be set up (Polesye, North-Western) as would unite all the local workers, Jewish as well as non-Jewish, into a single whole. At the Third Congress of the R.S.D.L.P. a resolution was adopted providing for the publication of literature in Yiddish. In fulfilment of that resolution we are now issuing a complete translation into Yiddish of the Report on the Third Congress of the R.S.D.L.P., which has appeared in Russian. The Report will show the Jewish workers—both those who are now in our Party and those who are temporarily out of it—how our Party is progressing. The Report will show the Jewish workers that our Party is already emerging from the internal crisis from which it has been suffering since the Second Congress. It will show them what the actual aspirations of our Party are and what its attitude is towards the Social-Democratic parties and organizations of the other nationalities, as well as the attitude of the entire Party and its central body to its component parts. Finally, it will show them—and this is most important—the tactical directives that were drawn up by the Third Congress of the R.S.D.L.P. with regard to the policy of the entire class-conscious proletariat in the present revolutionary situation.

Comrades! The hour of political struggle against the tsarist autocracy is drawing near—the struggle of the proletariat for the freedom of all classes and peoples in Russia, for freedom of the proletarian drive towards socialism. Terrible trials are in store for us. The outcome of the revolution in Russia depends on our class-consciousness and preparedness, on our unity and determination. Let us set to work then with greater boldness and greater unity, let us do all in our power for the proletarians of the different nationalities to march to freedom under the leadership of a really united Russian Social-Democratic Labor Party.

Editorial Board of the Central Organ
of the Russian Social-Democratic Labor Party

Written at the end
of May (beginning of June) 1905

First published in 1905 as a
preface to the pamphlet:
Report on the Third Congress of the
R.S.D.L.P.
(issued in Yiddish)

Published according to
the text of the pamphlet
translated from the Yiddish

REACTION IS TAKING TO ARMS

The Social-Democratic press has long been pointing out that the vaunted "constitutionalism" in Russia is baseless and ephemeral. So long as the old authority remains and controls the whole vast machinery of state administration, it is useless talking seriously about the importance of popular representation and about satisfying the urgent needs of the vast masses of the people. No sooner had the State Duma begun its sittings—and liberal-bourgeois oratory about peaceful, constitutional evolution burst forth in a particularly turbulent flood—than there began an increasing number of attacks on peaceful demonstrators, cases of setting fire to halls where public meetings were proceeding, and lastly, downright pogroms—all organized by government agents.

Meanwhile the peasant movement is growing. Strikes among the workers are becoming more embittered, more frequent and more extensive. Unrest is growing among the most backward military units, the infantry in the provinces, and among the Cossacks.

Far too much inflammable material has accumulated in Russian social life. The struggle which ages of unprecedented violence, torment, torture, robbery and exploitation have paved the way for has become too widespread and cannot be confined within the limits of a struggle of the Duma for a particular Ministry. Even the most downtrodden and ignorant "subjects" can no longer be restrained from proclaiming the demands of awakening human and civic dignity. The old authority, which has always made the laws itself, which in fighting for its existence is resorting to the last, most desperate, savage and furious methods, cannot be restrained by appeals to abide by the law.

The pogrom in Belostok is a particularly striking indication that the government has taken to arms against the people. The old, but ever new story of Russian pogroms!—*ever,* until the people achieve victory, until the old authorities are completely swept away. Here are a few excerpts from a telegram received from a Belostok elector, Tsirin: "A *deliberately-organized* anti-Jewish pogrom has started." "In spite of rumors that have been circulated, *not a single order has been received* from the Ministry all day today!" "Vigorous agitation for the pogrom has been carried on for the past two weeks. In the streets, particularly at night, leaflets were distributed calling for the massacre, not only of Jews, but also of intellectuals. *The police simply turned a blind eye to all this.*"

The old familiar picture! The police organizes the pogrom beforehand. The police instigates it: leaflets are printed in government printing offices calling for a massacre of the Jews. When the pogrom begins, the police is inactive. The troops quietly look on at the exploits of the Black Hundreds. But later this very police goes through the farce of prosecution and trial of the pogromists. The investigations and trials conducted by the officials of the old authority always end in the same way: the cases drag on, none of the pogromists are found guilty, sometimes even the battered and mutilated Jews and intellectuals are dragged before the court, months pass—and the old, but ever new story is forgotten, until the next pogrom. Vile instigation, bribery, and fuddling with drink of the scum of our cursed capitalist "civilization," the brutal massacre of unarmed by armed people, and farcical trials conducted by the culprits themselves! And yet there are those who, seeing these phenomena of Russian social life, think, and say, that somebody or other is "recklessly" calling upon the people to resort to "extreme measures"! One must be, not reckless, but a poltroon, politically corrupt, to say such things in the face of events like the burning of the People's House at Vologda (at the time of the opening of the Duma) or the pogrom in Belostok (after the Duma had been in session a month). A single event like this will have more effect upon the people than millions of appeals. And to talk about "reckless" appeals is just as hopelessly pedantic and as much a sin of a deadened civic conscience, as to condemn the wild cry for revenge that is going up from the battlefields of Vologda and Belostok.

The Duma did the right thing by immediately discussing the interpellation on the Belostok pogrom, and sending some of its members to Belostok to investigate on the spot. But in reading this interpellation, and comparing it with the speeches of members of the Duma and the commonly-known facts about progroms, one has a deep feeling of dissatisfaction, of indignation at the irresolute terms in which the interpellation is worded.

Judge for yourselves. The authors of the interpellation say: "The inhabitants *fear* that the local authorities and malicious agitators may try to make out the victims themselves to be responsible for the calamity that has befallen them." Yes, the downtrodden and tormented Jewish population is indeed apprehensive of this, and has *every* reason to be. This is true. But it is *not the whole truth*, gentlemen, members of the Duma, and authors of the interpellation! You, the people's deputies, who have not yet been assaulted and tormented, know perfectly well that this is not the whole truth. You know that the downtrodden inhabitants will *not dare* to name those who are *really responsible* for the pogrom. *You must name them.* That is what you are people's deputies for. That is why you enjoy even under Russian law—*complete* freedom of speech in the Duma. Then don't stand *between* the reaction and the people, at a time when the armed reaction is strangling, massacring, and mutilating unarmed people. Take your stand *openly and entirely* on the side of the people. Don't confine yourselves to conveying the fear of the townspeople that the vile instigators of the pogroms will say it is the murdered victims who are to blame. *Indict the culprits in unequivocal terms*—it is your direct *duty* to the people. Don't ask the government whether measures are being taken to protect the Jews and to prevent pogroms, but ask how long the government intends to shield the real culprits, who are members of the government. Ask the government whether it thinks that the people will long be in error as to who is really responsible for the pogroms. Indict the government openly and publicly; as the *only* means of protection against pogroms.

This is not in keeping with "parliamentary practice," you will say. Are you not ashamed to advance such an argument *even* at a time like this? Don't you realize that the people will condemn you if, even at a time like this, you do not give up playing at parliaments and do not dare to say straightforwardly, openly and loudly what *you really know and think?*

That you know the truth about the pogroms is evident from speeches delivered by members of the Duma. The Cadet Nabokov said: "We know that in many cases the administration has not succeeded in allaying the suspicion that the simultaneous outbreak of the pogroms is the result either of the Black-Hundred organizations operating *with the knowledge of the local authorities,* or, at best, of the latter's systematic inaction."

If you *know* that this is so, gentlemen of the Cadet Party, you should have said so in your interpellation. You should have written: We *know* such-and-such facts and therefore ask questions about them. And if you know what happens "at best," it is *unseemly* for people's deputies to keep silent about what happens at *worst,* about the deliberate organization of pogroms by the police on orders from St. Petersburg.

"Belostok is not an exceptional case," rightly said Levin. "It is one of the consequences of the system that you want to combat." Quite right, citizen Levin! But while in newspapers we can only speak of the "system," you in the Duma ought to speak out more plainly and sharply.

"Pogroms are part of a whole system. In the October days . . . the government . . . found no other means of combating the liberation movement . . . You know how that chapter of history ended. Now the same thing repeated. . . . This system is *perfidiously* prepared and thought out, and is being carried out *with equal perfidy.* In many cases we know very well who organizes these pogroms; we know very well that leaflets *are sent out by the gendarmerie departments.*"

Once again, quite right, citizen Levin! And therefore you should have said in your interpellation: does the government think that the Duma is not aware of the commonly-known fact that the gendarmes and police send out those leaflets?

Deputy Ryzhkov bluntly stated that the allegation that pogroms are due to racial enmity was a lie, and that the allegation that they were due to the impotence of the authorities was a malicious invention. Deputy Ryzhkov listed a number of facts which proved that there had been "collaboration" between the police, the pogromists and the Cossacks. "I live in a big industrial district," he said, "and I know that the pogrom in Lugansk, for example, did not assume ghastly dimensions *only because* [mark this, gentlemen: *only* because] the *unarmed workers* drove back the pogromists with their bare fists, at the risk of being shot by the police."

In *Rech,* this part of the report of the debate in the Duma is headed "The Government Is Indicted." This is a good heading, but it belongs in the *text of* the Duma *interpellation*, not in a newspaper report. Either draft these interpellations in such a way as to make them a passionate indictment of the government before the people, or in a way that they may arouse ironical taunts and jeers at the crying discrepancy between the monstrous facts and the bureaucratic evasions in bureaucratically-restrained interpellations. Only by adopting the first-mentioned method will the Duma teach the reactionaries not to jeer at it. As it is, the reactionaries are jeering, quite openly and frankly. Read today's *Novoye Vremya*. These lackeys of the pogromists are chuckling and making merry: "One cannot help observing with particular satisfaction [!!] the haste with which the Duma interpellated the Minister on the anti-Jewish pogrom in Belostok." You see: the pogromists are particularly pleased—the flunkey blurts out the truth. The reactionaries are pleased with the Belostok pogrom, and with the fact that they can now abusively call the Duma the "Jewish" Duma. The reactionaries jeer and say: "If as was stated in the Duma today, we must pardon the riots against property made by the peasants in the Russian gubernias, then we must also pardon the pogroms against Jewish property in the Western territory."

You see, gentlemen of the Duma, the reactionaries are more outspoken than you are. Their language is stronger than your Duma language. The reactionaries are not afraid to fight. They are not afraid to associate the Duma with the peasants' struggle for freedom. *Then don't you be afraid to associate the reactionary government with the pogromists!*

Written on June 3 (16), 1906
Published in *Vperyod*, No. 9,
June 4, 1906

Published according
to the newspaper text

UNION OF THE BUND WITH THE RUSSIAN
SOCIAL-DEMOCRATIC LABOR PARTY

The Seventh Congress of the Bund, the organization of the Jewish Social-Democratic workers of Russia, has recently taken place. According to the reports of this Congress, the total number of members of the Bund amounts to 33,000 in 257 organizations. Representation at the Congress was organized on a democratic basis, with one delegate for each 300 members of the Party. About 23,000 members took part in the elections and they sent to the Congress 68 delegates with the right to speak and vote.

The chief question that the Congress had to decide was that of the union of the Bund with the Russian Social-Democratic Labor Party. As is known, the Unity Congress of the R.S.D.L.P. pronounced in favor of unification and laid down the conditions for it, The Seventh Congress of the Bund has now accepted these conditions. Union with the R.S.D.L.P. was adopted by 48 votes against 20. Thus, the Russian Social-Democratic Labor Party has at last become a truly all-Russian and united organization. The membership of our Party is now *over 100,000*: 31,000 were represented at the Unity Congress, and then there are about 26,000 Polish Social-Democrats, about 14,000 Lettish and 33,000 Jewish Social-Democrats.

Representatives of the Central Committee of the Bund joined the Central Committee of the R.S.D.L.P. The rather difficult work of unifying the local organizations of the Bund and those of the R.S.D.L.P. now lies ahead.

The second question discussed at the Bund Congress was that of the present political situation. In a detailed resolution, adopted by a large majority of votes, the Seventh Congress of the Bund accepted *the convocation of a constituent assembly* as a tactical slogan, and rejected all reservations tending to weaken this slogan, such as "through the Duma", etc. Boycott of the Duma was rejected conditionally, that is to say, the necessity of taking part in the elections was recognized provided that the party of the proletariat was in a position to carry out an independent election campaign.

The third question was that of "guerrilla actions," without any division of them into "expropriations" and terrorist acts. By an overwhelming majority, a resolution *against* guerrilla actions was adopted.

The last question concerned the organization of the Bund. Organizational rules were adopted.

We limit ourselves to this short note for the time being; we hope in the near future to acquaint our readers more fully with the decisions of the Seventh Congress of the Bund.

Written in September 1906
First published in 1937
in *Lenin Miscellany XXX*

Published according to
the manuscript

SEPARATISTS IN RUSSIA
AND SEPARATISTS IN AUSTRIA

Among the various representatives of Marxism in Russia the Jewish Marxists, or, to be more exact, some of them—those known as the Bundists—are carrying out a policy of *separatism*. From the history of the working-class movement it is known that the Bundists *left the Party* in 1903, when the majority of the party of the working class refused to accept their demand to be recognized as the "sole" representatives of the Jewish proletariat.

This exit from the Party was a manifestation of separatism deeply harmful to the working-class movement. But, in fact, the Jewish workers have entered and continue to enter the Party everywhere in spite of the Bund. Side by side with the *separate* (isolated) organizations of the Bundists, there have *always* existed *general* organizations of the workers—Jewish, Russian, Polish, Lithuanian, Latvian, etc.

From the history of Marxism in Russia we know, furthermore, that when the Bund in 1906 again returned to the Party, the Party stipulated the condition that separatism should cease, i.e., that there should be local unity of *all* the Marxist workers of *whatever* nationality. But this condition *was not* fulfilled by the Bundists, despite its *special* confirmation by a special decision of the Party in December 1908.[20]

That, shortly, is the history of Bundist separatism in Russia. Unfortunately, it is little known to the workers, and little thought is given to it. Those having the closest practical acquaintance with this history are the Polish, the Lithuanian (especially in Vilna in 1907) and the Latvian Marxists (at the same time, in Riga), and the Marxists of South and Western Russia. It is well known, incidentally, that the Caucasian Marxists, including *all* the Caucasian Mensheviks, have until quite recently maintained local *unity* and even fusion of the workers of all nationalities, and have condemned the separatism of the Bundists.

We should also note that the prominent Bundist, Medem, in the well-known book, *Forms of the National Movement* (St. Petersburg, 1910), admits that the Bundists have never implemented unity in the localities, i.e., they have always been separatists.

In the international working-class movement, the question of separatism came to the front most urgently in 1910, at the Copenhagen Congress. The *Czechs* came forward as separatists in Austria, and destroyed the unity that had existed previously between the Czech and German workers. The International Congress at Copenhagen *unanimously* condemned separatism, but the Czechs have unfortunately remained separatists right up to the present.

Feeling themselves isolated in the proletarian International, the Czech separatists spent a long time searching unsuccessfully for supporters. Only now have they found some—in the *Bundists and liquidators*. The *čechoslavische Sozialdemokrat*, the bit of a journal published by the separatists in German, printed an article in its issue No. 3 (Prague, April 15, 1913) under the title "A Turn for the Better." this "turn" that is supposed to be for the "better" (actually, towards separatism) the Czech separatists saw—where do you think, reader? In *Nasha Zarya*, [21] the liquidators' journal, in an article by the *Bundist* V. Kossovsky!

At last the Czech separatists are not alone in the proletarian International! Naturally they are glad to be able to rope in even liquidators, even Bundists. But all class-conscious workers in Russia should give this fact some thought: the Czech separatists, unanimously condemned by the International, are clinging to the coat-tails of liquidators and Bundists.

Only the complete unity (in every locality, and from top to bottom) of the workers of all nations, which has existed so long and so successfully in the Caucasus, corresponds to the interests and tasks of the workers' movement.

Pravda No, 104,   Published according to
May 8, 1913   the *Pravda* text

THE WORKING CLASS AND
THE NATIONAL QUESTION

Russia is a motley country as far as her nationalities are concerned. Government policy, which is the policy of the landowners supported by the bourgeoisie, is steeped in Black-Hundred nationalism.

This policy is spearheaded against the *majority* of the peoples of Russia who constiture the *majority* of her population. And alongside this we have the bourgeois nationalism of other nations (Polish, Jewish, Ukrainian, Georgian, etc.), raising its head and trying *to divert* the working class from its great world-wide tasks by a national struggle or a struggle for national culture.

The national question must be clearly considered and solved by all class-conscious workers.

When the bourgeoisie was fighting for freedom together with the people, together with all those who labor, it stood for full freedom and equal rights for the nations. Advanced countries, Switzerland, Belgium, Norway and others, provide us with an example of how free nations under a really democratic system live together in peace or separate peacefully from each other.

Today the bourgeoisie fears the workers and is seeking an alliance with the Purishkeviches, with the reactionaries, and is betraying democracy, advocating oppression or unequal rights among nations and corrupting the workers with *nationalist* slogans.

In our times the proletariat alone upholds the real freedom of nations and the unity of workers of all nations.

For different nations to live together in peace and freedom or to separate and form different states (if that is more convenient for them), a full democracy, unheld by the working class, is essential. No privileges for any nation or any one language! Not even the slightest degree of oppression or the slightest injustice in respect of a national minority—such are the principles of working-class democracy.

The capitalists and landowners want, at all costs, to keep the workers of different nations apart while the powers-that-be live splendidly together as shareholders in profitable concerns involving millions (such as the Lena Goldfields); Orthodox Christians and Jews, Russians and Germans, Poles and Ukrainians, everyone who possesses *capital,* exploit the workers of all nations in company.

Class-conscious workers stand for *full unity* among the workers of all nations in every educational, trade union, political, etc., workers' organization. Let the Cadet gentlemen disgrace themselves by denying or belittling the importance of equal rights for Ukrainians. Let the bourgeoisie of all nations find comfort in lying phrases about national culture, national tasks, etc., etc.

The workers will not allow themselves to be disunited by sugary speeches about national culture, or "national-cultural autonomy." The workers of all nations together, concertedly, uphold full freedom and complete equality of rights in organizations common to all—and that is the guarantee of genuine culture.

The workers of the whole world are building up their own internationalist culture, which the champions of freedom and the enemies of oppression have for long been preparing. To the old world, the world of national oppression, national bickering, and national isolation the workers counterpose a new world, a world of the unity of the working people of all nations, a world in which there is no place for any privileges or for the slightest degree of oppression of man by man.

Pravda No. 106,   Published according to
May 10, 1913   the *Pravda* text

DRAFT PROGRAM OF THE FOURTH CONGRESS OF SOCIAL-DEMOCRATS OF THE LATVIAN AREA²² (Excerpt)

THE NATIONAL QUESTION

This question, both in its general theoretical, socialist presentation, and from the practical, organizational point of view (the organization of our own Party) is in urgent need of discussion and solution by all Social-Democratic organizations.

The liquidators' conference in August 1912—as was admitted even by the neutral Menshevik Plekhanov—*contravened* the Program of the R.S.D.L.P. in the spirit of *"adaptation of socialism to nationalism."*

In fact, this conference recognized, on the proposal of the Bund, the permissibility of the slogan of "cultural-national autonomy," which was contrary to the decision taken by the Second Party Congress.

This slogan (defended in Russia by *all the bourgeois* Jewish nationalist parties) contradicts the *internationalism* of Social-Democracy. As democrats, we are irreconcilably hostile to any, however slight, oppression of any nationality and to any privileges for any nationality. As democrats, we demand the right of nations to self-determination *in the political sense* of that term (see the Program of the R.S.D.L.P.), i.e., the right to secede. We demand unconditional *equality* for all nations in the state and the unconditional protection of the rights of every national minority. We demand broad self-government and autonomy for regions, which must be demarcated, among other terms of reference, in respect of nationality too.

All these demands are obligatory for every consistent democrat, to say nothing of a socialist.

Socialists, however, do not limit themselves to general democratic demands. They *fight* all possible manifestations of *bourgeois nationalism*, crude or refined. "National-cultural autonomy" is a manifestation precisely of this type—it *joins* the proletarians and bourgeoisie of *one* nation and *keeps* the proletarians of *different* nations *apart*.

Social-Democrats have always stood and still stand for the *internationalist* point of view. While protecting the equality of all nationalities against the serf-owners and the police state we do not support *"national culture"* but *international* culture, which includes only part of each national culture—only the consistently democratic and socialist content of each national culture.

The slogan of "national-cultural autonomy" deceives the workers with the phantom of a cultural unity of nations, whereas in every nation today a landowners', bourgeois or petty-bourgeois "culture" predominates.

We are against national culture as one of the slogans of bourgeois nationalism. *We are in favor of the international culture of a fully democratic and socialist proletariat.*

The unity of the workers of *all* nationalities coupled with the fullest equality for the nationalities and the most consistently democratic state system—that is our slogan, and it is the slogan of international revolutionary Social-Democracy. This truly proletarian slogan will not create the false phantom and illusion of "national" unity of the proletariat and the bourgeoisie, while the slogan of "national-cultural autonomy" undoubtedly does create that phantom and does sow that illusion among the working people.

We, Latvian Social-Democrats, living in an area with a population that is very mixed nationally, we, who are in an environment consisting of representatives of the bourgeois nationalism of the Letts, Russians, Estonians, Germans, etc., see with particular clarity the bourgeois falsity of the slogan of "cultural-national autonomy." The slogan of the *unity* of all and every organization of workers of *all* nationalities, tested in practice in our own Social-Democratic organization, is particularly dear to us.

Reference is frequently made to Austria in justification of the slogan of "national-cultural autonomy." As far as this reference is concerned it must be remembered that: first, the point of view of the chief Austrian theoretician on the national question, Otto

Bauer (in his book *The National Question and Social-Democracy*) has been recognized as an *exaggeration* of the national factor and a *terrible underestimation* of the international factor even by such a cautious writer as Karl Kautsky (see: K. Kautsky, *Nationalität und Internationalität*; it has been translated into Russian); secondly, in Russia *only* the Bund members, together with all Jewish bourgeois parties, have so far defended "cultural-national autonomy," whereas *neither* Bauer *nor* Kautsky *recognize* national autonomy for the Jews, and Kautsky (*op. cit.*) declares outright that the Jews of Eastern Europe (Galicia and Russia) are *a caste* and not a nation; thirdly, the Brünn* national program of the Austrian Social-Democratic Party (1899)[23] *does not* fully recognize extra-territorial (personal) national antonomy and goes only as far as to demand the union of all national regions of one nationality throughout the state (Sec. 3 of the Brünn Program); fourthly, even this program, obviously a compromise (and unsatisfactory from the standpoint of internationalism), was *a complete fiasco* in Austria itself, because the compromise did not bring peace but led, instead, to the secession of the Czech separatists; fifthly, these Czech separatists, unanimously condemned at the Copenhagen Congress by the entire International, declare the Bund type of separatism to be close to them (see: *Der čechoslavische Sozialdemokrat* No. 3, organ of the separatists, which may be obtained gratis from *Prague*: Praha, Hybernska 7); sixthly, Bauer himself demands the unity of Social-Democratic political organizations of various nationalities *in each locality*. Bauer himself considers the "national system" of the Austrian party, which has now led to a *complete* schism, to be unstable and contradictory.

In short, references to Austria speak *against* the Bund and not *in its favor*.

Unity from below, the complete unity and consolidation in each locality of Social-Democratic workers of all nationalities in all working-class organizations—that is our slogan. Down with the deceptive bourgeois, compromise slogan of "cultural-national autonomy"!

We are *against* federation in the structure of our Party, too, we are for the *unity* of local (and not only central) organizations of Social-Democrats of all nations.

The Congress must reject both the slogan of cultural-national autonomy and the principle of federation in the structure of the Party. The Latvian Social-Democrats, like Polish Social-Democrats, like the Social-Democrats of the Caucasus thoughout the period from 1898 to 1912 (for *14* whole years of Party history) must remain true to Social-Democratic internationalism.

Written in May 1913
First published in Lettish
as a separate reprint from
*Biletens Latwijas Sozialdemokratijas
Ahrsemju Grupu Biroma isdewums* No. 8
First published in Russian
in 1929 in the second and third editions
of V. I. Lenin's *Collected Works,* Vol. XVII

Published according to
the manuscript

HAS *PRAVDA* GIVEN PROOF
OF BUNDIST SEPARATISM?

Pravda No. 104 (308) published an article "Separatists in Russia and Separatists in Austria."* Now Mr. V. Kossovsky has published an article in *Luch* No. 119 (205) refuting it, or, to be more exact, containing a mass of vituperation against *Pravda* for that article. All we can do is draw the attention of the workers, who are interested in the fate of *their own* organization, to these slanging attacks by the *Luch* gentlemen, who *evade* the controversial questions.

What proof did *Pravda* offer of Bundist separatism?

1) The Bund *left the Party* in 1903. Mr. Kossovsky's invective did nothing to disprove this fact. The Kossovskys scold because they are *powerless* to disprove the facts.

2) Jewish workers have joined and are still joining the Party everywhere *in spite of the Bund.*

This poor defender of the Bund cannot say a word against that either!

3) The Bund has deliberately *contravened* the Party decision on the unity of workers, of *all nationalities* in local organizations, a decision that was taken in 1906 and given special confirmation in 1908.

Mr. Kossovsky *could not* say a word against that!

4) The Bundist Medem admitted that Bund members had never put into effect this unity in local organizations, that is, had always been separatists.

Again not a single objection from Mr. Kossovsky!

Just think of it, reader; what is the gentleman to do but scold and rage when he *cannot* say *a single word* against the *four* chief points in *Pravda?*

* See pp. 65-66.—*Ed.*

Pravda, furthermore, gave an exact quotation from the organ of the Czech separatists in Austria, who have been unanimously condemned for their separatism *by the entire* International. That organ *praises* Mr. Kossovsky (his article in the liquidators' *Nasha Zarya*) for his "turn for the better" in respect of the separatists.

Now what, Mr. Kossovsky? Is our quotation not correct? Mr. Kossovsky knows that it is, and is malicious in his impotence: "a review in some Czech news-sheet."

Don't lie, Mr. Separatist and Jewish liberal! Lies will not help you, for you will be exposed.

Not "a review" and not in "some Czech news-sheet," but a *special* article in the German *organ* of the Czech separatists.[24] This is a fact, and you have not refuted it.

I do not defend the separatists, says Mr. Kossovsky to justify himself, summarizing his article in *Nasha Zarya.*

Is that so? Then the *Czech separatists* have *misunderstood* you? The poor liberal leaders of the Bund! Not only their enemies, even their *friends "misunderstood"* them!

Any worker, however, will understand well enough that a petty liar who has been caught red-handed is seeking salvation in evasion and imprecation. You will not scare the workers that way, gentlemen.

Pravda has proved that the Bundists are separatists. Mr. V. Kossovsky has failed to refute it.

Messrs. Kossovsky, Medem & Co., are a group of liberal intellectuals that is corrupting the Jewish workers with bourgeois nationalism and separatism. For this reason *Pravda* has fought against and will continue to fight against the Bund.

Jewish Social-Democratic workers are joining the working-class party in spite of the Bund and against the Bund.

Pravda No. 127   Published according to
Signed: the *Pravda* text
June 5, 1913 Signed *V. I.*

THESES ON THE NATIONAL QUESTION[25]

1. The article of our program (on the self-determination of nations) cannot be interpreted to mean anything but *political* self-determination, i.e., the right to secede and form a separate state.

2. This article in the Social-Democratic program is *absolutely* essential to the Social-Democrats of Russia

a) for the sake of the basic principles of democracy in general;

b) also because there are, within the frontiers of Russia and, *what is more, in her frontier areas,* a number of nations with sharply distinctive economic, social and other conditions; furthermore, these nations (like all the nations of Russia except the Great Russians) are unbelievably oppressed by the tsarist monarchy;

c) lastly, also in view of the fact that throughout Eastern Europe (Austria and the Balkans) and in Asia—i.e., in countries bordering on Russia—the bourgeois-democratic reform of the state that has everywhere else in the world led, in varying degree, to the creation of independent national states or states with the closest, interrelated national composition, has either not been consummated or has only just begun;

d) at the present moment Russia is a country whose state system is more backward and reactionary than that of any of the contiguous countries, beginning—in the West—with Austria where the fundamentals of political liberty and a constitutional regime were consolidated in 1867, and where universal franchise has now been introduced, and ending—in the East—with republican China. In all their propaganda, therefore, the Social-Democrats of Russia must insist on the right of all nationalities to form separate states or to choose freely the state of which they wish to form part.

3. The Social-Democratic Party's recognition of the right of all nationalities to self-determination requires of Social-Democrats that they should *a)* be unconditionally hostile to the use of force in any form whatsoever by the dominant nation (or the nation which constitutes the majority of the population) in respect of a nation that wishes to secede politically.

b) demand the settlement of the question of such secession only on the basis of a universal, direct and equal vote of the population of the given territory by secret ballot;

c) conduct an implacable struggle against both the Black-Hundred-Octobrist and the liberal-bourgeois (Progressist, Cadet, etc.) parties on every occasion when they defend or sanction national oppression in general or the denial of the right of nations to self-determination in particular.

4. The Social-Democratic Party's recognition of the right of all nationalities to self-determination most certainly does not mean that Social-Democrats reject an independent appraisal of the advisability of the state secession of any nation in each separate case. Social-Democracy should, on the contrary, give its independent appraisal, taking into consideration the conditions of capitalist development and the oppression of the proletarians of various nations by the united bourgeoisie of all nationalities, as well as the general tasks of democracy, first of all and most of all the interests of the proletarian class struggle for socialism.

From this point of view the following circumstance must be given special attention. There are two nations in Russia that are more civilized and more isolated by virtue of a number of historical and social conditions and that could most easily and most "naturally" put into effect their right to secession. They are the peoples of Finland and Poland. The experience of the Revolution of 1905 has·shown that even in these two nations the ruling classes, the landowners and bourgeoisie, reject the revolutionary struggle for liberty and seek a *rapprochement* with the ruling classes of Russia and with the tsarist monarchy *because of their fear* of the revolutionary proletariat of Finland and Poland.

Social-Democracy, therefore, must give most emphatic warning to the proletariat and other working people of all nationalities against direct deception by the nationalistic slogans of "their own" bourgeoisie, who with their saccharine or fiery speeches about "our native land" try to *divide* the proletariat and *divert its attention* from their bourgeois intrigues while they enter into an economic and political alliance with the bourgeoisie of other nations and with the tsarist monarchy.

The proletariat cannot pursue its struggle for socialism and defend its everyday economic interests without the closest and fullest alliance of the workers of all nations in all working-class organizations without exception.

The proletariat cannot achieve freedom other than by revolutionary struggle for the overthrow of the tsarist monarchy and its replacement by a democratic republic. The tsarist monarchy *precludes* liberty and equal rights for nationalities, and is, furthermore, the bulwark of barbarity, brutality and reaction in both Europe and Asia. This monarchy can be overthrown only by the united proletariat of all the nations of Russia, which is giving the lead to consistently democratic elements capable of revolutionary struggle from among the working masses of all nations.

It follows, therefore, that workers who place political unity with "their own" bourgeoisie above complete unity with the proletariat of all nations, are acting against their own interests, against the interests of socialism and against the interests of democracy.

5. Social-Democrats, in upholding a consistently democratic state system, demand unconditional equality for all nationalities and struggle against absolutely all privileges for one or several nationalities.

In particular, Social-Democrats reject a "state" language. It is particularly superfluous in Russia because more than seven-tenths of the population of Russia belong to related Slav nationalities who, given a free school and a free state, could easily achieve intercourse by virtue of the demands of the economic turnover without any "state" privileges for any one language.

Social-Democrats demand the abolition of the old administrative divisions of Russia established by the feudal landowners and the civil servants of the autocratic feudal state and their replacement by divisions based on the requirements of present-day economic life and in accordance, as far as possible, with the national composition of the population.

All areas of the state that are distinguished by social peculiarities or by the national composition of the population, must enjoy wide self-government and autonomy, with institutions organized on the basis of universal, equal and secret voting.

6. Social-Democrats demand the promulgation of a law, operative throughout the state, protecting the rights of every national minority in no matter what part of the state. This law should declare inoperative any measure by means of which the national majority might attempt to establish privileges for itself or restrict the right of a national minority (in the sphere of education, in the use of any specific language, in budget affairs, etc.), and forbid the implementation of any such measure by making it a punishable offense.

7. The Social-Democratic attitude to the slogan of "cultural-national" (or simply "national") "autonomy" or to plans for its implementation is a negative one, since this slogan (1) undoubtedly contradicts the internationalism of the class struggle of the proletariat, (2) makes it easier for the proletariat and the masses of working people to be drawn into the sphere of influence of bourgeois nationalism, and (3) is capable of distracting attention from the task of the consistent democratic transformation of the state as a whole, which transformation alone can ensure (to the extent that this can, in general, be ensured under capitalism) peace between nationalities.

In view of the special acuteness of the question of cultural-national autonomy among Social-Democrats, we give some explanation of the situation.

a) It is impermissible, from the standpoint of Social-Democracy, to issue the slogan of *national* culture either directly or indirectly. The slogan is incorrect because already under capitalism, all economic, political and spiritual life is becoming more and more international. Socialism will make it completely international. International culture, which is now already being systematically created by the proletariat of all countries, does not absorb "national culture" (no matter of what national group) as a whole, but accepts from *each* national culture *exclusively* those of its elements that are consistently democratic and socialist.

b) Probably the one example of an approximation, even though it is a timid one, to the slogan of national culture in Social-Democratic program is Article 3 of the Brünn Programme of the Austrian Social-Democrats. This Article 3 reads: "All self-governing regions of one and the same nation form a single-national alliance that has complete autonomy in deciding its national affairs."

This is a compromise slogan since it does not contain a shadow of extra-territorial (personal) national autonomy. But this slogan, too, is erroneous and harmful, for it is no business of the Social-Democrats of Russia to unite into one nation the Germans in Lodz, Riga, St. Petersburg and Saratov. Our business is to struggle for full democracy and the annulment of *all* national privileges and to unite the German workers in Russia with the workers of all other nations in upholding and developing the international culture of socialism.

Still more erroneous is the slogan of extra-territorial (personal) national autonomy with the setting up (according to a plan drawn up by the consistent supporters of this slogan) of national parliaments and national state secretaries (Otto Bauer and Karl Renner). Such institutions contradict the economic conditions of the capitalist countries, they have not been tested in any of the world's democratic states and are the opportunist dream of people who despair of setting up consistent democratic institutions and are seeking salvation from the national squabbles of the bourgeoisie in the artificial isolation of the proletariat and the bourgeoisie of each nation on a number of ("cultural") questions.

Circumstances occasionally compel Social-Democrats to submit for a time to some sort of compromise decisions, but from other countries we must borrow not compromise decisions, but consistently Social-Democratic decisions. It would be particularly unwise to adopt the unhappy Austrian compromise decision today, when it had been a complete failure in Austria and has led to the separatism and secession of the Czech Social-Democrats.

c) The history of the "cultural-national autonomy" slogan in Russia shows that it has been adopted by *all* Jewish bourgeois parties and *only* by Jewish bourgeois parties; and that they have been uncritically followed by the Bund, which has inconsistently rejected the national-Jewish parliament (sejm) and national-Jewish state secretaries. Incidentally, even those European Social-Democrats who accede to or defend the compromise slogan of cultural-national autonomy, admit that the slogan is quite unrealizable for the Jews (Otto Bauer and Karl Kautsky). "The Jews in Galicia and Russia are more of a caste than a nation, and attempts to constitute Jewry as a nation are attempts at preserving a caste" (Karl Kautsky).

d) In civilized countries we observe a fairly full (relatively) approximation to national peace under capitalism *only* in conditions of the *maximum* implementation of democracy throughout the state system and administration (Switzerland). The slogans of consistent democracy (the republic, a militia, civil servants elected by the people, etc.) unite the proletariat and the working people, and, in general, all progressive elements in each nation in the name of the struggle for conditions that preclude even the slightest national privilege—while the slogan of "cultural-national autonomy" preaches the isolation of nations in educational affairs (or "cultural" affairs, in general), an isolation that is quite compatible with the retention of the grounds for all (including national) privileges.

The slogans of consistent democracy *unite* in a single whole the proletariat and the advanced democrats of all nations (elements that demand not isolation but the uniting of democratic elements of the nations in all matters, including educational affairs), while the slogan of cultural-national autonomy *divides* the proletariat of the different nations and links it up with the reactionary and bourgeois elements of the separate nations.

The slogans of consistent democracy are implacably hostile to the reactionaries and to the counter-revolutionary bourgeoisie of all nations, while the slogan of cultural-national autonomy is quite acceptable to the reactionaries and counter-revolutionary bourgeoisie of some nations.

8. The sum-total of economic and political conditions in Russia therefore demands that Social-Democracy should *unite* unconditionally workers of all nationalities in *all* proletarian organizations without exception (political, trade union, co-operative, educational, etc., etc.). The Party should not be federative in structure and should not form national Social-Democratic groups but should unite the proletarians of all nations in the given locality, conduct propaganda and agitation in *all* the languages of the local proletariat, promote the common struggle of the workers of all nations against every kind of national privilege and should recognize the autonomy of local and regional Party organizations.

9. More than ten years' experience gained by the R.S.D.L.P. confirms the correctness of the above thesis. The Party was founded in 1898 as a party of all Russia, that is, a party of the proletariat of all the nationalities of Russia. The Party remained "Russian" when the Bund seceded in 1903, after the Party Congress had rejected the demand to consider the Bund the *only* representative of the Jewish proletariat. In 1906 and 1907 events showed convincingly that there were no grounds for this demand, a large number of Jewish proletarians continued to co-operate in the common Social-Democratic work in many local organizations, and the Bund re-entered the Party. The Stockholm Congress (1906) brought into the Party the Polish and Latvian Social-Democrats, who favored *territorial* autonomy, and the Congress, furthermore, did *not* accept the principle of federation and demanded unity of Social-Democrats of all nationalities in each locality. This principle has been in operation in the Caucasus for many years, it is in operation in Warsaw (Polish workers and Russian soldiers), in Vilna (Polish, Lettish, Jewish and Lithuanian workers) and in Riga, and in the three last-named places it has been implemented *against* the separatist Bund. In December 1908, the R.S.D.L.P., through its conference, adopted a special resolution confirming the demand for the *unity* of workers of all nationalities, *on a principle other than* federation. The splitting activities of the Bund separatists in the fulfilling the Party decision led to the collapse of all that "federation of the worst type"[26] and brought about the *rapprochement* of the Bund and the Czech separatists and vice versa (see Kossovsky in *Nasha Zarya* and the organ of the Czech separatists, *Der čechoslavische Sozialdemokrat* No. 3, 1913, on Kossovsky), and, lastly, at the August (1912) Conference of the liquidators it led to an *undercover* attempt by the Bund separatists and liquidators and some of the Caucasian liquidators to insert "cultural-national autonomy" into the Party program *without any defense of its substance!*

Revolutionary worker Social-Democrats in Poland, in the Latvian Area and in the Caucasus still stand for territorial autonomy and the *unity* of worker Social-Democrats of *all* nations. The Bund-liquidator secession and the alliance of the Bund with *non*-Social-Democrats in Warsaw place the *entire* national question, both in its theoretical aspect and in the matter of Party structure, *on the order of the day* for all Social-Democrats.

Compromise decisions have been broken by the very people

who introduced them against the will of the Party, and the demand for the unity of worker Social-Democrats of all nationalities is being made more loudly than ever.

10. The crudely militant and Black-Hundred-type nationalism of the tsarist monarchy, and also the revival of *bourgeois* nationalism—Great-Russian (Mr. Struve, *Russkaya Molva*,[27] the Progressists, etc.), the Ukrainian, and Polish (the anti-Semitism of Narodowa "Demokracja"[28]), and Georgian and Armenian, etc.—all this makes it particularly urgent for Social-Democratic organizations in all parts of Russia to devote greater attention than before to the national question and to work out consistently Marxist decisions on this subject in the spirit of consistent internationalism and unity of proletarians of all nations.

*   *   *

a*) The slogan of national culture is incorrect and expresses only the limited bourgeois understanding of the national question. International culture.

b*) The perpetuation of national divisions and the promoting of refined nationalism—unification, *rapprochement,* the mingling of nations and the expression of the principles of a *different,* international culture.

c*) The despair of the petty bourgeois (hopeless struggle against national bickering) and the fear of radical-democratic reforms and the socialist movement—only radical-democratic reforms can establish national peace in capitalist states and only socialism is able to terminate national bickering.

d*) National curias in educational affairs.[29]

e*) The Jews.

Written in June 1913   Published according to
First published in 1925   the manuscript
in the *Lenin Miscellany III*

---

* These letters are in Greek in the manuscript.

THE NATIONALIZATION
OF JEWISH SCHOOLS

The politics of the government are soaked in the spirit of nationalism. Attempts are made to confer every kind of privilege upon the "ruling," i.e., the Great-Russian nation, even though the Great Russians represent a *minority* of the population of Russia, to be exact, only 43 per cent.

Attempts are made to cut down still further the rights of all the other nations inhabiting Russia, to segregate one from the other and stir up enmity among them.

The extreme expression of present-day nationalism is the scheme for the nationalization of Jewish schools. The scheme emanated from the educational officer of Odessa district, and has been sympathetically considered by the Ministry of Public "Education." What does this nationalization mean?

It means segregating the Jews into *special* Jewish schools (secondary schools). The doors of all other educational establishments —both private and state—are to be completely closed to the Jews. This "brilliant" plan is rounded off by the proposal to limit the number of pupils in the Jewish secondary schools to the notorious "quota"!

In all European countries such measures and laws against the Jews existed only in the dark centuries of the Middle Ages, with their Inquisition, the burning of heretics and similar delights. In Europe the Jews have long since been granted complete equality and are fusing more and more with the nations in whose midst they live.

The most harmful feature in our political life generally, and in the above scheme particularly, apart from the oppression and persecution of the Jews, is the striving to fan the flames of nationalism, to segregate the nationalities in the state one from another, to increase their estrangement, to separate their schools.

The interests of the working class—as well as the interests of political liberty generally—require, on the contrary, the fullest equality of all the nationalities in the state without exception, and the elimination of every kind of barrier between the nations, the bringing together of children of all nations in the same schools, etc. Only by casting off every savage and foolish national prejudice, only by uniting the workers of all nations into one association, can the working class become a force, offer resistance to capitalism, and achieve a serious improvement in its living conditions.

Look at the capitalists! They try to inflame national strife among the "common people," while they themselves manage their business affairs remarkably well—Russians, Ukrainians, Poles, Jews, and Germans together in one and the same corporation. Against the workers the capitalists of all nations and religions are united, but they strive to divide and weaken the workers by national strife!

This most harmful scheme for the nationalization of the Jewish schools shows, incidentally, how mistaken is the plan for so-called "cultural-national autonomy," i.e., the idea of taking education out of the hands of the state and handing it over to each nation separately. It is not this we should strive for, but for the unity of the workers of all nations in the struggle against *all* nationalism, in the struggle for a truly democratic *common* school and for political liberty generally. The example of the advanced countries of the world—say, Switzerland in Western Europe or Finland in Eastern Europe—shows us that only consistently-democratic state institutions ensure the most peaceable and human (not bestial) coexistence of various nationalities, *without* the artificial and harmful separation of education according to nationalities.

Severnaya Pravda No. 14
August 18, 1913
Signed: *V. I.*

Published according to
the *Severnaya Pravda* text

RESOLUTIONS OF THE SUMMER, 1913 JOINT CONFERENCE OF THE CENTRAL COMMITTEE OF THE R.S.D.L.P. AND PARTY OFFICIALS (Excerpt)[30]

The orgy of Black-Hundred nationalism, the growth of nationalist tendencies among the liberal bourgeoisie and the growth of nationalist tendencies among the upper classes of the oppressed nationalities, give prominence at the present time to the national question.

The state of affairs in the Social-Democratic movement (the attempts of the Caucasian Social-Democrats, the Bund and the liquidators to annul the Party Program,[31] etc.) compels the Party to devote more attention than ever to this question.

This Conference, taking its stand on the Program of the R.S.D.L.P., and in order to organize correctly Social-Democratic agitation on the national question, advances the following propositions:

1. Insofar as national peace is in any way possible in a capitalist society based on exploitation, profit-making and strife, it is attainable only under a consistently and thoroughly democratic republican system of government which guarantees full equality of all nations and languages, which recognizes no compulsory official language, which provides the people with schools where instruction is given in all the native languages, and the constitution of which contains a fundamental law that prohibits any privileges whatsoever to any one nation and any encroachment whatsoever upon the rights of a national minority. This particularly calls for wide regional autonomy and fully democratic local self-government, with the boundaries of the self-governing and autonomous regions determined by the local inhabitants themselves on the basis of

their economic and social conditions, national make-up of the population, etc.

2. The division of the educational affairs of a single state according to nationalities is undoubtedly harmful from the standpoint of democracy in general, and of the interest of the proletarian class struggle in particular. It is precisely this division that is implied in the plan for "cultural-national" autonomy, or for "the creation of institutions that will guarantee freedom for national development" adopted in Russia by all the Jewish bourgeois parties and by the petty-bourgeois, opportunist elements among the different nations.

3. The interests of the working class demand the amalgamation of the workers of all the nationalities in a given state in united proletarian organizations—political, trade union, cooperative, educational, etc. This amalgamation of the workers of different nationalities in single organizations will alone enable the proletariat to wage a victorious struggle against international capital and reaction, and combat the propaganda and aspirations of the landowners, clergy and bourgeois nationalists of all nations, who usually cover up their anti-proletarian aspirations with the slogan of "national culture." The world working-class movement is creating and daily developing more and more an international proletarian culture.

4. As regards the right of the nations oppressed by the tsarist monarchy to self-determination, i.e., the right to secede and form independent states, the Social-Democratic Party must unquestionably champion this right. This is dictated by the fundamental principles of international democracy in general, and specifically by the unprecedented national oppression of the majority of the inhabitants of Russia by the tsarist monarchy, which is a most reactionary and barbarous state compared with its neighboring states in Europe and Asia. Furthermore, this is dictated by the struggle of the Great-Russian inhabitants themselves for freedom, for it will be impossible for them to create a democratic state if they do not eradicate Black-Hundred, Great-Russian nationalism, which is backed by the traditions of a number of bloody suppressions of national movements and systematically fostered not only by the tsarist monarchy and all the reactionary parties, but also by the Great-Russian bourgeois liberals, who toady to the monarchy, particularly in the period of counter-revolution.

5. The right of nations to self-determination (i.e., the constitutional guarantee of an absolutely free and democratic method of deciding the question of secession) must under no circumstances be confused with the expediency of a given nation's secession. The Social-Democratic Party must decide the latter question exclusively on its merits in each particular case in conformity with the interests of social development as a whole and with the interests of the proletarian class struggle for socialism.

Social-Democrats must moreover bear in mind that the landowners, the clergy and the bourgeoise of the oppressed nations often cover up with nationalist slogans their efforts to divide the workers and dupe them by doing deals behind their backs with the landowners and bourgeoisie of the ruling nation to the detriment of the masses of the working people of all nations.

* * *

This Conference places on the agenda of the Party congress the question of the national program. It invites the Central Committee, the Party press and the local organizations to discuss (in pamphlets, debates, etc.) the national question in fullest detail.

Written September 1913
Published in 1913 in the pamphlet
*Notification and Resolutions
of the Summer, 1913,
Joint Conference of the Central
Committee of the R.S.D.L.P.
and Party Officials.*
Issued by the Central Committee

Published according to
the text of the illegal
mimeographed edition
of the resolutions collated
with the text of the pamphlet

"CULTURAL-NATIONAL" AUTONOMY

The essence of the plan, or program, of what is called "cultural-national" autonomy (or: "the establishment of institutions that will guarantee freedom of national development") is *separate schools for each nationality.*

The more often all avowed and tacit nationalists (including the Bundists) attempt to obscure this fact the more we must insist on it.

Every nation, irrespective of place of domicile of its individual members (irrespective of territory, hence the term "extra-territorial" autonomy) is a united officially recognized association conducting national-cultural affairs. The most important of these affairs is education. The determination of the composition of the nations by allowing every citizen to register freely, irrespective of place of domicile, as belonging to any national association, ensures absolute precision and absolute consistency in segregating the schools according to nationality.

Is such a division, be it asked, permissible from the point of view of democracy in general, and from the point of view of the interests of the proletarian class struggle in particular?

A clear grasp of the essence of the "cultural-national autonomy" program is sufficient to enable one to reply without hesitation—it is absolutely impermissible.

As long as different nations live in a single state they are bound to one another by millions and thousands of millions of economic, legal and social bonds. How can education be extricated from these bonds? Can it be "taken out of the jurisdiction" of the state, to quote the Bund formula, classical in its striking absurdity? If the various nations living in a single state are bound by economic ties, then any attempt to divide them permanently in "cultural" and particularly educational matters would be absurd and reactionary.

88

On the contrary, effort should be made to *unite* the nations in educational matters, so that the schools should be a preparation for what is actually done in real life. At the present time we see that the different nations are unequal in the rights they possess and in their level of development. Under these circumstances, segregating the schools according to nationality would *actually* and inevitably *worsen* the conditions of the more backward nations. In the southern, former slave states of America, Negro children are still segregated in separate schools, whereas in the North, white and Negro children attend the same schools. In Russia a plan was recently proposed for the "nationalization of Jewish schools," i.e., the segregation of Jewish children from the children of other nationalities in separate schools. It is needless to add that this plan originated in the most reactionary, Purishkevich circles.

One cannot be a democrat and at the same time advocate the principle of segregating the schools according to nationality. Note: we are arguing at present from the general democratic (i.e., bourgeois-democratic) point of view.

From the point of view of the proletarian class struggle we must oppose segregating the schools according to nationality far more emphatically. Who does not know that the capitalists of all the nations in a given state are most closely and intimately united in joint-stock companies, cartels and trusts, in manufacturers' associations, etc., which are directed *against* the workers irrespective of their nationality? Who does not know that in *any* capitalist undertaking—from huge works, mines and factories and commercial enterprises down to capitalist farms—we *always*, without exception, see a larger variety of nationalities among the workers than in remote, peaceful and sleepy villages?

The urban workers, who are best acquainted with developed capitalism and perceive more profoundly the psychology of the class struggle—their whole life teaches them or they perhaps imbibe it with their mothers' milk—such workers instinctively and inevitably realize that segregating the schools according to nationality is not only a *harmful* scheme, but a downright fraudulent swindle on the part *of the capitalists*. The workers *can* be split up, divided and weakened by the advocacy of such in idea, and still more by the segregation of the ordinary peoples' schools according to nationality; while the capitalists, whose children are well provided with rich private schools and specially engaged tutors, *cannot in any way* be threatened by any division of weakening through "cultural-national autonomy."

As a matter of fact, "cultural-national autonomy," i.e., the absolutely pure and consistent segregating of education according to nationality, was invented not by the capitalists *(for the time being* they resort to cruder methods to divide the workers) but by the opportunist, philistine intelligentsia of Austria. There is *not a trace* of this brilliantly philistine and brilliantly nationalist idea in any of the democratic West-European countries with mixed populations. This idea of the despairing petty bourgeois could arise only in Eastern Europe, in backward, feudal, clerical, bureaucratic Austria, where *all* public and political life is hampered by wretched, petty squabbling (worse still: cursing and brawling) over the question of languages. Since cat and dog can't agree, let us at least segregate all the nations once and for all absolutely clearly and consistently in "national curias" for educational purposes!—such is the psychology that engendered this foolish idea of "cultural-national autonomy." The proletariat, which is conscious of and cherishes its internationalism, will never accept this nonsense of refined nationalism.

It is no accident that in Russia this idea of "cultural-national autonomy" was accepted *only by all* the Jewish bourgeois parties, then (in 1907) by the conference of the *petty-bourgeois* Left-Narodnik parties of different nationalities, and lastly by the petty-bourgeois, opportunist elements of the *near-Marxist* groups, i.e., the Bundists and the liquidators (the latter were even too timid to do so straightforwardly and definitely). It is no accident that in the State Duma *only* the semi-liquidator Chkhenkeli, who is infected with nationalism, and the petty bourgeois Kerensky, spoke in favor of "cultural-national autonomy."

In general, it is quite funny to read the liquidator and Bundist references to Austria on this question. First of all, why should the most backward of the multinational countries be taken as the *model?* Why not take the most advanced? This is very much in the style of the bad Russian liberals, the Cadets, who for models of a constitution turn mainly to such backward countries as Prussia and Austria, and not to advanced countries like France, Switzerland and America!

Secondly, after taking the Austrian model, the Russian nationalist philistines, i.e., the Bundists, liquidators, Left Narodniks, and so forth, have themselves changed it *for the worse*. In this country it is the Bundists (plus *all* the Jewish bourgeois parties, in whose wake the Bundists follow without always realizing it) that mainly and primarily use this plan for "cultural-national autonomy" in their propaganda and agitation; and yet in Austria, the country where this idea of "cultural-national autonomy" originated, Otto Bauer, the father of the idea, devoted a special chapter of his book to proving that "cultural-national autonomy" *cannot* be applied to the Jews!

This proves more conclusively than lengthy speeches how inconsistent Otto Bauer is and how little he believes in his own idea, for he excludes the *only* extra-territorial (not having its own territory) nation from his plan for extra-territorial national autonomy.

This shows how Bundists borrow *old-fashioned* plans from Europe, multiply the mistakes of Europe tenfold and "develop" them to the point of absurdity.

The fact is—and this is the third point—that at their congress in Brünn (in 1899) the Austrian Social-Democrats *rejected* the program of "cultural-national autonomy" that was proposed to them. They merely adopted a compromise in the form of a proposal for a union of the nationally delimited *regions* of the country. This compromise did *not* provide either for extra-territoriality or for segregating education according to nationality. In accordance with this compromise, in the most advanced (capitalistically) populated centers, towns, factory and mining districts, large country estates, etc., there are *no* separate schools for each nationality!

The Russian working class has been combating this reactionary, pernicious, petty-bourgeois nationalist idea of "cultural-national autonomy," and will continue to do so.

Za Pravdu No. 46,   Published according to
November 28, 1913   the *Za Pravdu* text

THE NATIONALITY OF PUPILS
IN RUSSIAN SCHOOLS

To obtain a more precise idea of the plan for "cultural-national autonomy," which boils down to segregating the schools according to nationality, it is useful to take the concrete data which show the nationality of the pupils attending Russian schools. For the St. Petersburg educational area such data are provided by the returns of the school census taken on January 18, 1911.

The following are the data on the distribution of pupils attending elementary schools under the Ministry of Public Education according to the *native languages* of the pupils. The data cover the whole of the St. Petersburg educational area, but *in brackets* we give the *figures for* the city of St. Petersburg. Under the term "Russian language" the officials constantly lump together Great-Russian, Byelorussian and Ukrainian ("Little Russian," according to official terminology). Total pupils—265,660 (48,076).

Russian—232,618 (44,223); Polish—1,737 (780); Czech—3 (2); Lithuanian—84 (35); Lettish—1,371 (113); Zhmud—1 (0); French—14 (13); Italian—4 (4); Rumanian—2 (2); German—2,408 (845); Swedish—228 (217); Norwegian—31 (0); Danish—1 (1); Dutch—1 (0); English—8 (7); Armenian—3 (3); Gypsy— 4 (0); Jewish—1,196 (396); Georgian—2 (1); Ossetian—1 (0); Finnish—10,750 (874); Karelian—3,998 (2); Chud—247 (0); Estonian—4,723 (536); Lapp—9 (0); Zyryan—6,008 (0); Samoyed—5 (0); Tatar—63 (13); Persian—1 (1); Chinese—1 (1); not ascertained—138 (7).

These are comparatively accurate figures. They show that the national composition of the population is extremely mixed, although they apply to one of the basically Great-Russian districts of Russia. The extremely mixed national composition of the population of the large city of St. Petersburg is at once evident. This is no accident, but results from a *law* of capitalism that operates in all countries and in all parts of the world. Large cities, factory, metal-lurgical, railway and commercial and industrial centers generally, are certain, more than any other, to have very mixed populations, and it is precisely these centers that grow faster than all others and constantly attract larger and larger numbers of the inhabitants of the backward rural areas.

Now try to apply to these real-life data the lifeless utopia of the nationalist philistines called "cultural-national autonomy" or (in the language of the Bundists) "taking out of the jurisdiction of the state" questions of national culture, i.e., primarily educational af-fairs.

Educational affairs "shall be taken out of the jurisdiction of the state" and transferred to 23 (in St. Petersburg) "national associa-tions" each developing "its own" "national culture"!

It would be ridiculous to waste words to prove the absurdity and reactionary nature of a "national program" of this sort.

Is is as clear as daylight that the advocacy of such a plan means, *in fact*, pursuing or supporting the ideas of bourgeois nationalism, chauvinism and clericalism. The interests of democracy in general, and the interests of the working class in particular, demand the very opposite. We must strive to secure the *mixing* of the children of *all* nationalities in *uniform* schools in each locality; the workers of all nationalities must *jointly* pursue the proletarian educational policy which Samoilov, the deputy of the Vladimir workers, so ably formulated on behalf of the Russian Social-Democratic workers' group in the State Duma.[32] We must emphatically oppose seg-regating the schools according to nationality, no matter what form it may take.

It is not our business to segregate the nations in matters of edu-cation in any way; on the contrary, we must strive to create the fundamental democratic conditions for the peaceful coexistence of the nations on the basis of equal rights. We must not champion "national culture," but expose the clerical and bourgeois character of this slogan in the name of the international culture of the world working-class movement.

But we may be asked whether it is possible to safeguard the interests of the *one* Georgian child among the 48,076 schoolchil-dren in St. Petersburg on the basis of equal rights. And we would reply that it is impossible to establish a special Georgian school in

St. Petersburg on the basis of Georgian "national culture," and that
to advocate such a plan means sowing *pernicious* ideas among the
masses of the people.

But we shall not be defending anything harmful, of be striving
after anything that is impossible, if we demand for this child free
government premises for lectures on the Georgian language,
Georgian history, etc., the provision of Georgian books from the
Central Library for this child, a state contribution towards the fees
of the Georgian teacher, and so forth. Under real democracy,
when bureaucracy and "Peredonovism"[33] are completely eliminated from the schools, the people can quite easily achieve this.
But this real democracy can be achieved *only* when the workers of
all nationalities are united.

To preach the establishment of special national schools for every
"national culture" is reactionary. But under real democracy it is
quite possible to ensure instruction in the native language, in native history and so forth, *without* splitting up the schools according
to nationality. And complete local self-government will make it
impossible for anything to be forced upon the people, as for example, upon the 713 Karelian children in Kem Uyezd (where there
are only 514 Russian children) or upon the 681 Zyryan children in
Pechora Uyezd (153 Russian), or upon the 167 Lettish children in
Novgorod Uyezd (over 7,000·Russian), and so on and so forth.

Advocacy of impracticable cultural-national autonomy is an absurdity, which now already is only disuniting the workers ideologically. To advocate the amalgamation of the workers of all
nationalities means facilitating the success of proletarian class solidarity, which will guarantee equal rights for, and maximum peaceful coexistence of, all nationalities.

Proletarskaya Pravda No. 7,   Published according to
December 14, 1913   the *Proletarskaya Pravda* text

THE NATIONAL PROGRAM
OF THE R.S.D.L.P. (Excerpt)

The Conference of the Central Committee has adopted a resolution on the national question,* which has been printed in the "Notification," and has placed the question of a national program on the agenda of the Congress.

Why and how the national question has, at the present time, been brought to the fore—in the entire policy of the counter-revolution, in the class-consciousness of the bourgeoisie and in the proletarian Social-Democratic Party of Russia—is shown in detail in the resolution, itself. There is hardly any need to dwell on this in view of the clarity of the situation. This situation and the fundamentals of a national progrm for Social-Democracy have recently been dealt with in Marxist theoretical literature (the most prominent place being taken by Stalin's article[34]). We therefore consider that it will be to the point if, in this article, we confine ourselves to the presentation of the problem from a purely Party standpoint and to explanations that cannot be made in the legal press, crushed as it is by the Stolypin-Maklakov oppression.

Social-Democracy in Russia is taking shape by drawing exclusively on the experience of older countries, i.e., of Europe, and on the theoretical expression of that experience, Marxism. The specific features of our country and the specific features of the historical period of the establishment of Social-Democracy in our country are: first, in our country, as distinct from Europe, Social-Democracy began to take shape *before* the bourgeois revolution and continued taking shape *during* that revolution. Secondly, in our country the inevitable struggle to separate proletarian from general bourgeois and petty-bourgeois democracy—a struggle that is fundamentally the same as that experienced by every country

* See pp. 85-87.

—is being conducted under the conditions of a complete theoretical victory of Marxism in the West and in our country. The form taken by this struggle, therefore, is not so much that of a struggle for Marxism as a struggle for or against petty-bourgeois theories that are hidden behind "almost Marxist" phrases.

That is how the matter stands, beginning with Economism (1895-1901) and "legal Marxism" (1895-1901, 1902). Only those who shrink from historical truth can forget the close, intimate connection and relationship between these trends and Menshevism (1903-07) and liquidationism (1908-13).

In the national question the old *Iskra*, which in 1901-03 worked on and completed a program for the R.S.D.L.P. as well as laying the first and fundamental basis of Marxism in the theory and practice of the Russian working class movement, had to struggle, in the same way as on other questions, against petty-bourgeois opportunism. This opportunism was expressed, first and foremost, in the nationalist tendencies and waverings of the Bund. The old *Iskra* conducted a stubborn struggle against Bund nationalism, and to forget this is tantamount to becoming a Forgetful John again, and cutting oneself off from the historical and ideological roots of the whole Social-Democratic workers' movement in Russia.

On the other hand, when the Program of the R.S.D.L.P. was finally adopted at the Second Congress in August 1903, there was a struggle, unrecorded in the Minutes of the Congress because it took place in the *Program Commission*, which was visited by almost the entire Congress—a struggle against the clumsy attempts of several Polish Social-Democrats to cast doubts on "the right of nations to self-determination," i.e., attempts to deviate towards opportunism and nationalism from a quite different angle.

And today, ten years later, the struggle goes on along those same two basic *lines*, which shows equally that there is a profound connection between this struggle and all the objective conditions affecting the national question in Russia.

At the Brünn Congress in Austria (1899) the program of "cultural-national autonomy" (defended by Kristan, Ellenbogen and others and expressed in the draft of the Southern Slavs) was *rejected*. *Territorial* national autonomy was adopted, and Social-Democratic propaganda for the obligatory union of all national regions was only a *compromise* with the idea of "cultural-national autonomy." The chief theoreticians of this unfortunate idea themselves lay particular emphasis on its *inapplicability* to Jewry.

In Russia—*as usual*—people have been found who have made it their business to enlarge on a little opportunist error and develop it into a system of opportunist policy. In the same way as Bernstein in Germany brought into being the Right Constitutional-Democrats in Russia—Struve, Bulgakov, Tugan & Co.—so Otto Bauer's "forgetfulness of internationalism" (as the supercautious Kautsky calls it!) *gave rise* in Russia to the *complete* acceptance of "cultural-national autonomy" *by all* the Jewish bourgeois parties and a large number of petty-bourgeois trends (the Bund and a *conference* of Socialist-Revolutionary national parties in 1907). Backward Russia serves, one might say, as an example of how the microbes of West-European opportunism produce whole *epidemics* on our savage soil.

In Russia people are fond of saying that Bernstein is "tolerated" in Europe, but they forget to add that nowhere in the world, with the exception of "holy" Mother Russia, has Bernsteinism engendered Struvism,[35] or has "Bauerism" led to the justification, by Social-Democrats, of the refined nationalism of the Jewish bourgeoisie.

"Cultural-national autonomy" implies precisely the most refined and, therefore, the most harmful nationalism, it implies the corruption of the workers by means of the slogan of national culture and the propaganda of the profoundly harmful and even anti-democratic segregating of schools according to nationality. In short, this program undoubtedly contradicts the internationalism of the proletariat and is in accordance only with the ideals of the nationalist petty bourgeoise.

Sotsial-Demokrat No. 32,   Published according to
December 15 (28), 1913   the *Sotsial-Demokrat* text

ONCE MORE ON THE SEGREGATION
OF THE SCHOOLS ACCORDING
TO NATIONALITY

Marxists resolutely oppose nationalism in all its forms, from the crude reactionary nationalism of our ruling circles and of the Right Octobrist parties, down to the more or less refined and disguised nationalism of the bourgeois and petty-bourgeois parties.

Reactionary, or Black-Hundred, nationalism strives to safeguard the privileges of one nation, condemning all other nations to an inferior status, with fewer rights, or even with no rights at all. Not a single Marxist, and not even a single democrat, can treat this nationalism with anything else but the utmost hostility.

In words, bourgeois and bourgeois-democratic nationalists recognize the equality of nations, but in deeds they (often covertly, behind the backs of the people) stand for certain privileges for one of the nations, and always try to secure greater advantages of "their own" nation (i.e., for the bourgeoisie of their own nation); they strive to separate and segregate nations, to foster national exclusiveness, etc. By talking most of all about "national culture" and emphasizing what separates one nation from the other, bourgeois nationalists *divide the workers* of the various nations and fool them with "nationalist slogans."

The class-conscious workers combat *all* national oppression and *all* national privileges, but they do not confine themselves to that. They combat all, even the most refined, nationalism, and advocate not only the unity, but also the *amalgamation* of the workers of *all* nationalities in the struggle against reaction and against bourgeois nationalism in all its forms. Our task is not to segregate nations, but to unite the workers of all nations. Our banner does not carry the slogan "national culture" but *international* culture, which unites all the nations in a higher, socialist unity, and the way to which is already being paved by the international amalgamation of capital.

The influence of petty bourgeois, philistine nationalism has infected certain "would-be socialists," who advocate what is called "cultural-educational autonomy," i.e., the transfer of educational affairs (and matters of national culture in general) from the state to the individual nations. Naturally, Marxists combat this propaganda for the *segregation of nations*, they combat this refined nationalism, they combat the *segregating of the schools according to nationality*. When our Bundists, and later, the liquidators, wanted to support "cultural-national autonomy" *in direct opposition to* our Program, they were condemned not only by the Bolsheviks, but also by the pro-Party Mensheviks (Plekhanov).

Now Mr. An, in *Novaya Rabochaya Gazeta* (No. 103) is trying to defend a bad case by subterfuge, and by showering abuse upon us. We calmly ignore the abuse; it is merely a sign of the liquidators' feebleness.

To have schools conducted in the native languages—this, Mr. An assures us, is what is meant by segregating the schools according to the nationalities of the pupils; the *Pravda* people, he says, want to deprive the non-Russians of their national schools!

We can afford to laugh at this trick of Mr. An's, for everybody knows that *Pravda* stands for the fullest equality of languages, and even for the abolition of an official language! Mr. An's impotent rage is causing him to lose his head. This is dangerous, dear Mr. An!

The right of a nation to use its native language is explicitly and definitely recognized in § 8 of the Marxist program.[36]

If Mr. An is right in stating that having schools conducted in the native languages means segregating the schools according to nationality, why did the Bundists in 1906, and the liquidators in 1912, "supplement" (or rather, *distort)* the Program adopted in 1903—at the very Congress which *rejected* "cultural-national autonomy"—which *fully* recognizes the right of a nation to use its *native language*?

Your subterfuge will fail, Mr. An, and you will not succeed in covering up with your noise, clamor and abuse the fact that the liquidators have *violated* this Program, and that they have "adapted socialism to nationalism," as Comrade Plekhanov expressed it.

We do not want to have the Program violated. We do not want socialism to be adapted to nationalism. We stand for complete democracy, for the complete freedom and equality of languages, but give no support whatever to the proposal to "transfer educational affairs to the nations" or to "segregate schools according to nationality."

"The question at issue is that of segregating the schools according to nations," writes Mr. An, "hence, these nations must exist in each locality, hindering each other's development; and consequently, *they must be segregated* in the sphere of public education as well."

The words we have emphasized clearly reveal how liquidationism is dragging Mr. An away from socialism towards nationalism. The *segregation* of nations within the limits of a single state is harmful, and we Marxists strive *to bring the nations together and to amalgamate them.* Our object is not to "segregate" nations, but to secure for them, through full democracy, an equality and coexistence as peaceful (relatively) as in Switzerland.*

Proletarskaya Pravda No. 9,   Published according
December 17, 1913   the *Proletarskaya Pravda* text

---

* Mr. An boldly asserts that "there is no intermixing of nations even in the cantons of Switzerland." Will he not blush if we mention *four* cantons: Berne, Fribourg, Graubünden and Valais?

CRITICAL REMARKS
ON THE NATIONAL QUESTION[37] (Excerpts)

1. LIBERALS AND DEMOCRATS ON THE LANGUAGE QUESTION

On several occasions the newspapers have mentioned the report of
the Governor of the Caucasus, a report that is noteworthy, not for
its Black-Hundred[38] spirit, but for its timid "liberalism." Among
other things, the Governor objects to artificial Russification of
non-Russian nationalities. Representatives of non-Russian
nationalities in the Caucasus are *themselves* striving to teach their
children Russian; an example of this is the Armenian church
schools, in which the teaching of Russian is now obligatory.

Russkoye Solvo[39] (No. 198), one of the most widely circulating
liberal newspapers in Russia, points to this fact and draws the correct conclusion that the hostility towards the Russian language in
Russia "stems exclusively from" the "artificial" (it should have said
"forced") implanting of that language.

"There is no reason to worry about the fate of the Russian language. It will itself win recognition throughout Russia," says the
newspaper. This is perfectly true, because the requirements of
economic exchange will always compel the nationalities living in
one state (as long as they wish to live together) to study the language of the majority. The more democratic the political system in
Russia becomes, the more powerfully, rapidly and extensively
capitalism will develop, the more urgently will the requirements of
economic exchange impel various nationalities to study the language most convenient for general commercial relations.

The liberal newspaper, however, hastens to slap itself in the face
and demonstrate its liberal inconsistency.

"Even those who oppose Russification," it says, "would hardly
be likely to deny that in a country as huge as Russia there must be

one single official language, and that this language can be only Russian."

Logic turned inside out! Tiny Switzerland has not lost anything, but has gained from having not *one single* official language, but three—German, French and Italian. In Switzerland 70 per cent of the population are Germans (in Russia 43 per cent are Great Russians), 22 per cent French (in Russia 17 per cent are Ukrainians) and 7 per cent Italians (in Russia 6 per cent are Poles and 4.5 per cent Byelorussians). If Italians in Switzerland often speak French in their common parliament they do not do so because they are menaced by some savage police law (there are none such in Switzerland), but because the civilized citizens of a democratic state themselves prefer a language that is understood by a majority. The French language does not instil hatred in Italians because it is the language of a free civilized nation, a language that is not imposed by disgusting police measures.

Why should "huge" Russia, a much more varied and terribly backward country, *inhibit* her development by the retention of any kind of privilege for any one language? Should not the contrary be true, liberal gentlemen? Should not Russia, if she wants to overtake Europe, put an end to every kind of privilege as quickly as possible, as completely as possible and as vigorously as possible?

If all privileges disappear, if the imposition of any one language ceases, all Slavs will easily and rapidly learn to understand each other and will not be frightened by the "horrible" thought that speeches in different languages will be heard in the common parliament. The requirements of economic exchange will themselves *decide* which language of the given country it is to the *advantage* of the majority to know in the interests of commercial relations. This decision will be all the firmer because it is adopted voluntarily by a population of various nationalities, and its adoption will be the more rapid and extensive the more consistent the democracy and, as a consequence of it, the more rapid the development of capitalism.

The liberals approach the language question in the same way as they approach all political questions—like hypocritical hucksters, holding out one hand (openly) to democracy and the other (behind their backs) to the feudalists and police. We are against privileges, shout the liberals, and under cover they haggle with the feudalists for first one, then another, privilege.

Such is the nature of *all* liberal-bourgeois nationalism—not only Great-Russian (it is the worst of them all because of its violent character and its kinship with the Purishkeviches[40]), but Polish, Jewish, Ukrainian, Georgian and every other nationalism. Under the slogan of "national culture" the bourgeoisie of *all* nations, both in Austria and in Russia, are *in fact* pursuing the policy of splitting the workers, emasculating democracy and haggling with the feudalists over the sale of the people's rights and the people's liberty.

The slogan of working-class democracy is not "national culture" but the international culture of democracy and the world-wide working-class movement. Let the bourgeoisie deceive the people with various "positive" national programs. The class-conscious worker will answer the bourgeoisie —there is only one solution to the national problem (insofar as it can, in general, be solved in the capitalist world, the world of profit, squabbling and exploitation), and that solution is consistent democracy.

The proof—Switzerland in Western Europe, a country with an old culture and Finland in Eastern Europe, a country with a young culture.

The national program of working-class democracy is: absolutely no privileges for any one nation or any one language; the solution of the problem of the political self-determination of nations, that is, their separation as states by completely free, democratic methods; the promulgation of a law for the whole state by virtue of which any measure (rural, urban or communal, etc., etc.,) introducing any privilege of any kind for one of the nations and militating against the equality of nations or the rights of a national minority, shall be declared illegal and ineffective, and any citizen of the state shall have the right to demand that such a measure be annulled as unconstitutional, and that those who attempt to put it into effect be punished.

Working-class democracy contraposes to the nationalist wrangling of the various bourgeois parties over questions of language, etc., the demand for the unconditional unity and complete amalgamation of workers of *all* nationalities in *all* working-class organizations—trade union, co-operative, consumers', educational and all others—in contradistinction to any kind of bourgeois nationalism. Only this type of unity and amalgamation can uphold democracy and defend the interests of the workers against capital—which is already international and is becoming more so——and promote the development of mankind towards a new way of life that is alien to all privileges and all exploitation.

2. "NATIONAL CULTURE"

As the reader will see, the article in *Severnaya Pravda*, made use of a particular example, i.e., the problem of the official language, to illustrate the inconsistency and opportunism of the liberal bourgeoisie, which, in the national question, extends a hand to the feudalists and the police. Everybody will understand that, apart from the problem of an official language, the liberal bourgeoisie behaves just as treacherously, hypocritically and stupidly (even from the standpoint of the interests of liberalism) in a number of other related issues.

The conclusion to be drawn from this? It is that *all* liberal-bourgeois nationalism sows the greatest corruption among the workers and does immense harm to the cause of freedom and the proletarian class struggle. This bourgeois (and bourgeois-feudalist) tendency is all the more dangerous for its *being concealed* behind the slogan of "national culture." It is under the guise of national culture—Great-Russian, Polish, Jewish, Ukrainian, and so forth——that the Black-Hundreds and the clericals, and also the bourgeoisie of *all* nations, are doing their dirty and reactionary work.

Such are the facts of the national life of today, if viewed from the Marxist angle, i.e., from the standpoint of the class struggle, and if the slogans are compared with the interests and policies of classes, and not with meaningless "general principles," declamations and phrases.

The slogan of national culture is a bourgeois (and often also a Black-Hundred and clerical) fraud. Our slogan is: the international culture of democracy and of the world working-class movement.

Here the Bundist Mr. Liebman rushes into the fray and annihilates me with the following deadly tirade:

"Anyone in the least familiar with the national question knows that international culture is not non-national culture (culture without a national form); non-national culture, which must not be Russian, Jewish or Polish, but only pure culture, is nonsense; international ideas can appeal to the working class only when they are adapted to the language spoken by the worker, and to the concrete national conditions under which he lives; the worker should not be indifferent to the condition and development of his national culture, because it is through it, and only through it, that he is able to participate in the 'international culture of democracy and of the world working-class movement.' This is well known, but V.I. turns a deaf ear to it all. . . ."

Ponder over this typically Bundist argument, designed, if you please, to demolish the Marxist thesis that I advanced. With the air of supreme self-confidence of one who is "familiar with the national question," this Bundist passes off ordinary bourgeois views as "well-known" axioms.

It is true, my dear Bundist, that international culture is not non-national. Nobody said that it was. Nobody has proclaimed a "pure" culture, either Polish, Jewish, or Russian, etc., and your jumble of empty words is simply an attempt to distract the reader's attention and to obscure the issue with tinkling words.

The *elements* of democratic and socialist culture are present, if only in rudimentary form, in *every* national culture, since in *every* nation there are toiling and exploited masses, whose conditions of life inevitably give rise to the ideology of democracy and socialism. But *every* nation also possesses a bourgeois culture (and most nations a reactionary and clerical culture as well) in the form, not merely of "elements", but of the *dominant* culture. Therefore, the general "national culture" *is* the culture of the landlords, the clergy and the bourgeoisie. This fundamental and, for a Marxist, elementary truth, was kept in the background by the Bundist, who "drowned" it in his jumble of words, i.e., *instead of* revealing and clarifying the class gulf to the reader, he in fact obscured it. *In fact*, the Bundist acted like a bourgeois, whose every interest requires the spreading of a belief in a non-class national culture.

In advancing the slogan of "the international culture of democracy and of the world working-class movement," we take *from each* national culture *only* its democratic and socialist elements; we take them *only* and *absolutely* in opposition to the bourgeois culture and the bourgeois nationalism of *each* nation. No democrat, and certainly no Marxist, denies that all languages should have equal status, or that it is necessary to polemize with one's "native" bourgeoisie in one's native language and to advocate anti-clerical or anti-bourgeois ideas among one's "native" peasantry and petty bourgeoisie. That goes without saying, but the Bundist uses these indisputable truths to obscure the point in dispute, i.e., the real issue.

The question is whether it is permissible for a Marxist, directly or indirectly, to advance the slogan of national culture, or whether he should *oppose* it by advocating, in all languages, the slogan of workers' *internationalism* while "adapting" himself to all local and national features.

The significance of the "national culture" slogan is not determined by some petty intellectual's promise, or good intention, to "interpret" it as "meaning the development through it of an international culture." It would be puerile subjectivism to look at it in that way. The significance of the slogan of national culture is determined by the objective alignment of all classes in a given country, and in all countries of the world. The national culture of the bourgeoisie is a *fact* (and, I repeat, the bourgeoisie everywhere enters into deals with the landed proprietors and the clergy). Aggressive bourgeois nationalism, which drugs the minds of the workers, stultifies and disunites them in order that the bourgeoisie may lead them by the halter—such is the fundamental fact of the times.

Those who seek to serve the proletariat must unite the workers of all nations, and unswervingly fight bourgeois nationalism, *domestic* and foreign. The place of those who advocate the slogan of national culture is among the nationalist petty bourgeois, not among the Marxists.

Take a concrete example. Can a Great-Russian Marxist accept the slogan of national, Great-Russian, culture? No, he cannot. Anyone who does that should stand in the ranks of the nationalists, not of the Marxists. Our task is to fight the dominant, Black-Hundred and bourgeois national culture of the Great Russians, and to develop, exclusively in the internationalist spirit and in the closest alliance with the workers of other countries, the rudiments also existing in the history of our democratic and working-class movement. Fight your own Great-Russian landlords and bourgeoisie, fight their "culture" in the name of internationalism, and, in so fighting, "adapt" yourself to the special features of the Purishkeviches and Struves—that is your task, not preaching or tolerating the slogan of national culture.

The same applies to the most oppressed and persecuted nation—the Jews. Jewish national culture is the slogan of the rabbis and the bourgeoisie, the slogan of our enemies. But there are other elements in Jewish culture and in Jewish history as a whole. Of the ten and a half million Jews in the world, somewhat over half live in Galicia and Russia, backward and semi-barbarous countries, where the Jews are *forcibly* kept in the status of a caste. The other half lives in the civilized world, and there the Jews do not live as a segregated caste. There the great world-progressive features of Jewish culture stand clearly revealed: its internationalism, its identification with the advanced movements of the epoch (the percentage of Jews in the democratic and proletarian movements is everywhere higher than the percentage of Jews among the population).

Whoever, directly or indirectly, puts forward the slogan of Jewish "national culture" is (whatever his good intentions may be) an enemy of the proletariat, a supporter of all that is *outmoded* and connected with *caste* among the Jewish people; he is an accomplice of the rabbis and the bourgeoisie. On the other hand, those Jewish Marxists who mingle with the Russian, Lithuanian, Ukrainian and other workers in international Marxist organizations, and make their contribution (both in Russian and in Yiddish) towards creating the international culture of the working-class movement—these Jews, despite the separatism of the Bund, uphold the best traditions of Jewry by fighting the slogan of "national culture."

Bourgeois nationalism and proletarian internationalism —these are the two irreconcilably hostile slogans that correspond to the two great class camps throughout the capitalist world, and express the *two* policies (nay, the two world outlooks) in the national question. In advocating the slogan of national culture and building up on it an entire plan and practical program of what they call "cultural-national autonomy," the Bundists are *in effect* instruments of bourgeois nationalism among the workers.

3. THE NATIONALIST BOGEY OF "ASSIMILATION"

The question of assimilation, i.e., of the shedding of national features, and absorption by another nation, strikingly illustrates the consequences of the nationalist vacillations of the Bundists and their fellow-thinkers.

Mr. Liebman, who faithfully conveys and repeats the stock arguments, or rather, tricks, of the Bundists, has qualified as "the *old assimilation story*" the demand for the unity and amalgamation of the workers of all nationalities in a given country in united workers' organizations (see the concluding part of the article in *Severnaya Pravda*).

"Consequently," says Mr. F. Liebman, commenting on the concluding part of the article in *Severnaya Pravda*, "if asked what nationality he belongs to, the worker must answer: I am a Social-Democrat."

Our Bundist considers this the acme of wit. As a matter of fact, he gives himself away completely by *such* witticisms and outcries about "assimilation," *levelled against* a consistently democratic and *Marxist* slogan.

Developing capitalism knows two historical tendencies in the national question. The first is the awakening of national oppression, and the creation of national states. The second is the development and growing frequency of international intercourse in every form, the breakdown of national barriers, the creation of the international unity of capital, of economic life in general, of politics, science, etc.

Both tendencies are a universal law of capitalism. The former predominates in the beginning of its development, the latter characterizes a mature capitalism that is moving towards its transformation into socialist society. The Marxists' national program takes both tendencies into account, and advocates, firstly, the equality of nations and languages and the impermissibility of all *privileges* in this respect (and also the right of nations to self-determination, with which we shall deal separately later); secondly, the principle of internationalism and uncompromising struggle against contamination of the proletariat with bourgeois nationalism, even of the most refined kind.

The question arises: what does our Bundist mean when he cries out to heaven against "assimilation"? He *could not* have meant the oppression of nations, or the *privileges* enjoyed by a particular nation, because the word "assimilation" here does not fit at all, because all Marxists, individually, and as as official, united whole, have quite definitely and unambiguously condemned the slightest violence against and oppression and inequality of nations, and finally because this general Marxist idea, which the Bundist has attacked, is expressed in the *Severnaya Pravda* article in the most emphatic manner.

No, evasion is impossible here. In condemning "assimilation" Mr. Liebman had in mind, *not* violence, *not* inequality, and *not* privileges. Is there anything real left in the concept of assimilation, after all violence and all inequality have been eliminated?

Yes, there undoubtedly is. What is left is capitalism's world-historical tendency to break down national barriers, obliterate national distinctions, and to *assimilate* nations—a tendency which manifests itself more and more powerfully with every passing decade, and is one of the greatest driving forces transforming capitalism into socialism.

Whoever does not recognize and champion the equality of nations and languages, and does not fight against all national oppression or inequality, is not a Marxist; he is not even a democrat. That is beyond doubt. But it is also beyond doubt that the pseudo-Marxist who heaps abuse upon a Marxist of another nation for being an "assimilator" is simply a *nationalist philistine.* In this unhandsome category of people are all the Bundists and (as we shall shortly see) Ukrainian nationalist-socialists such as L. Yurkevich, Donstov and Co.

To show concretely how reactionary the views held by these nationalist philistines are, we shall cite facts of three kinds.

It is the Jewish nationalists in Russia in general, and the Bundists in particular, who vociferate most about Russian orthodox Marxists being "assimilators." And yet, as the afore-mentioned figures show, out of the ten and a half million Jews all over the world, *about half* that number live in the *civilized* world, where conditions favoring "assimilation" are *strongest*, whereas the unhappy, downtrodden, disfranchised Jews in Russia and Galicia, who are crushed under the heel of the Purishkeviches (Russian and Polish), live where conditions for "assimilation" *least* prevail, where there is most segregation, and even a "Pale of Settlement",[41] a *numerus clausus*[42] and other charming features of the Purishkevich regime.

The Jews in the civilized world are not a nation, they have in the main become assimilated, say Karl Kautsky and Otto Bauer. The Jews in Galicia and in Russia are not a nation; unfortunately (through *no* fault of their own but through that of the Purishkeviches), they are still a *caste* here. Such is the incontrovertible judgement of people who are undoubtedly familiar with the history of Jewry and take the above-cited facts into consideration.

What do these facts prove? It is that only Jewish reactionary philistines, who want to turn back the wheel of history, and make it proceed, not from the conditions prevailing in Russia and Galicia to those prevailing in Paris and New York, but in the reverse direction—only they can clamor against "assimilation."

The best Jews, those who are celebrated in world history, and have given the world foremost leaders of democracy and socialism, have never clamored against assimilation. It is only those who contemplate the "rear aspect" of Jewry with reverential awe that clamor against assimilation. . . .

4. "CULTURAL -NATIONAL AUTONOMY

The question of the "national culture" slogan is of enormous importance to Marxists, not only because it determines the ideological content of all our propaganda and agitation on the national question, as distinct from bourgeois propaganda, but also because the entire program of the much-discussed cultural-national autonomy is based on this slogan.

The main and fundamental flaw in this program is that it aims at introducing the most refined, most absolute and most extreme nationalism. The gist of this program is that every citizen registers as belonging to a particular nation, and every nation constitutes a legal entity with the right to impose compulsory taxation on its members, with national parliaments (Diets) and national secretaries of state (ministers).

Such an idea, applied to the national question, resembles Proudhon's idea, as applied to capitalism. Not abolishing capitalism and its basis—commodity production—but *purging* that basis of abuses, of excrescences, and so forth; not abolishing exchange and exchange value, but, on the contrary, making it "constitutional," universal, absolute, "*fair*," and free of fluctuations, crises and abuses—such was Proudhon's idea.

Just as Proudhon was petty-bourgeois, and his theory converted exchange and commodity production into an absolute category and exalted them as the acme of perfection, so is the theory and program of "cultural-national autonomy" petty bourgeois, for it converts bourgeois nationalism into an absolute category, exalts it as the acme of perfection, and purges it of violence, injustice, etc.

Marxism cannot be reconciled with nationalism, be it even of the "most just," "purest," most refined and civilized brand. In place of all forms of nationalism Marxism advances internationalism, the amalgamation of all nations in the higher unity, a unity that is growing before our eyes with every mile of railway line that is built, with every international trust, and every workers' association that is formed (an association that is international in its economic activities as well as in its ideas and aims).

The principle of nationality is historically inevitable in bourgeois society and, taking this society into due account, the Marxist fully recognizes the historical legitimacy of national movements. But to prevent this recognition from becoming an apologia of nationalism, it must be strictly limited to what is progressive in such movements, in order that this recognition may not lead to bourgeois ideology obscuring proletarian consciousness.

The awakening of the masses from feudal lethargy, and their struggle against all national oppression, for the sovereignty of the people, of the nation, are progressive. Hence, it is the Marxist's *bounden* duty to stand for the most resolute and consistent democratism on all aspects of the national question. This task is largely a

negative one. But this is the limit the proletariat can go to in supporting nationalism, for beyond that begins the "positive" activity
of the *bourgeoisie* striving to *fortify* nationalism.

To throw off the feudal yoke, all national oppression, and all
privileges enjoyed by any particular nation or language, is the im-
perative duty of the proletariat as a democratic force, and is certainly in the interests of the proletarian classstruggle, which is obscured and retarded by bickering on the national question. But to
go *beyond* these strictly limited and definite historical limits in
helping bourgeois nationalism means betraying the proletariat and
siding with the bourgeoisie. There is a border-line here, which is
often very slight and which the Bundists and Ukrainian
nationalist-socialists completely lose sight of.

Combat all national oppression? Yes, of course! Fight *for* any
kind of national development, *for* "national culture" in
general?—Of course not. The economic development of capitalist
society presents us with examples of immature national movements
all over the world, examples of the formation of big nations out of a
number of small ones, or to the detriment of some of the small
ones, and also examples of the assimilation of nations. The development of nationality in general is the principle of bourgeois
nationalism; hence the exclusiveness of bourgeois nationalism,
hence the endless national bickering. The proletariat, however, far
from undertaking to uphold the national development of every nation, on the contrary, warns the masses against such illusions,
stands for the fullest freedom of capitalist intercourse and wel-
comes every kind of assimilation of nations, except that which is
founded on force or privilege.

Consolidating nationalism within a certain "justly" delimited
sphere, "constitutionalizing" nationalism, and securing the separation of all nations from one another by means of a special state
institution—such is the ideological foundation and content of
cultural-national autonomy. This idea is thoroughly bourgeois and
thoroughly false. The proletariat cannot support any consecration
of nationalism; on the contrary, it supports everything that helps to
obliterate national distinctions and remove national barriers; it
supports everything that makes the ties between nationalities
closer and closer, or tends to merge nations. To act differently
means siding with reactionary nationalist philistinism.

When, at their Congress in Brünn[43] (in 1899), the Austrian Social-Democrats discussed the plan for cultural-national autonomy, practically no attention was paid to a theoretical appraisal of that plan. It is, however, noteworthy that the following two arguments were levelled against this program: (1) it would tend to strengthen clericalism; (2) "its result would be the perpetuation of chauvinism, its introduction into every small community, into every small group" (p. 92 of the official report of the Brünn Congress, in German. A Russian translation was published by the Jewish nationalist party, the J.S.L.P.[44]).

There can be no doubt that "national culture," in the ordinary sense of the term, i.e., schools, etc., is at present under the predominant influence of the clergy and the bourgeois chauvinists in all countries in the world. When the Bundists, in advocating "cultural-national" autonomy, say that the constituting of nations will keep the class struggle within them *clean* of all extraneous considerations, then that is manifest and ridiculous sophistry. It is primarily in the economic and political sphere that a serious class struggle is waged in any capitalist society. To separate the sphere of education *from this* is, firstly, absurdly utopian, because schools (like "national culture" in general) cannot be separated from economics and politics; secondly, it is the economic and political life of a capitalist country that *necessitates* at every step the smashing of the absurd and outmoded national barriers and prejudices, whereas separation of the school system and the like, would only perpetuate, intensify and strengthen "pure" clericalism and "pure" bourgeois chauvinism.

On the boards of joint-stock companies we find capitalists of different nations sitting together in complete harmony. At the factories workers of different nations work side by side. In any really serious and profound political issue sides are taken according to classes, not nations. Withdrawing school education and the like from state control of the nations is in effect an attempt to *separate* from economics, which unites the nations, the most highly, so to speak, ideological sphere of social life, the sphere in which "pure" national culture or the national cultivation of clericalism and chauvinism has the freest play.

In practice, the plan for "extra-territorial" or "cultural-national" autonomy could mean only one thing: *the division of educational affairs according to nationality*, i.e., the introduction of national curias in school affairs. Sufficient thought to the real significance of the famous Bund plan will enable one to realize how utterly reactionary it is even from the standpoint of democracy, let alone from that of the proletarian class struggle for socialism.

A single instance and a single scheme for the "nationalization" of the school system will make this point abundantly clear. In the United States of America the division of the states into northern and southern holds to this day in all departments of life; the former possess the greatest traditions of freedom and of struggle against the slave-owners; the latter possess the greatest traditions of slave-ownership, survivals of persecution of the Negroes, who are economically oppressed and culturally backward (44 per cent of Negroes are illiterate, and 6 per cent of whites), and so forth. In the northern states Negro children attend the same schools as white children do. In the South there are separate "national," or racial, which ever you please, schools for Negro children. I think that this is the sole instance of actual "nationalization" of schools.

In Eastern Europe there exists a country where things like the Beilis case[45] are still possible, and Jews are condemned by the Purishkeviches to a condition worse that that of the Negroes. In that country a scheme for *nationalizing Jewish schools* was recently mooted in the Ministry. Happily, this reactionary utopia is no more likely to be realized than the utopia of the Austrian petty bourgeoisie, who have despaired of achieving consistent democracy or of putting an end to national bickering, and have invented for the nations school-education *compartments* to keep them from bickering *over the distribution* of schools . . . but have "constituted" themselves for an *eternal* bickering of one "national culture" with another.

In Austria, the idea of cultural-national autonomy has remained largely a flight of literary fancy, which the Austrian Social-Democrats themselves have not taken seriously. In Russia, however, it has been incorporated in the programs of all the Jewish bourgeois parties, and of several petty-bourgeois, opportunist elements in the different nations—for example, the Bundists, the liquidators in the Caucasus, and the conference of Russian national parties of the Left-Narodnik trend. (This conference, we will mention parenthetically, took place in 1907, its decision being adopted *with abstention* on the part of the Russian Social-ist-Revolutionaries[46] and the P.S.P.,[47] the Polish social-patriots. Abstention from voting is a method surprisingly characteristic of the Socialist-Revolutionaries and P.S.P., when they want to show their attitude towards a most important question of principle in the sphere of the national program!)

In Austria it was Otto Bauer, the principal theoretician of "cultural-national autonomy," who devoted a special chapter of his book to prove that such a program cannot possibly be proposed for the Jews. In Russia, however, it is precisely among Jews that all the bourgeois parties—and the Bund which echoes them—have adopted this Program.* What does this go to show? It goes to show that history, through the political practice of another state, has exposed the absurdity of Bauer's invention, in exactly the same way as the Russian Bernsteinians (Struve, Tugan-Baranovsky, Berdayev and Co.), through their rapid evolution from Marxism to liberalism, exposed the real ideological content of the German Bernsteinism[50].

* * *

Since we have had to touch upon the Austrian program on the national question, we must reassert a truth which is often distorted by the Bundists. At the Brünn Congress a *pure* program of "cultural-national autonomy" *was* presented. This was the program of the South-Slav Social Democrats, §2 of which reads: "Every nation living in Austria, irrespective of the territory occupied by its members, constitutes an autonomous group which manages all its national (language and cultural) affairs quite independently." This

* That the Bundists often vehemently deny that *all* the Jewish bourgeois parties have accepted "cultural-national autonomy" is understandable. This fact only too glaringly exposes the actual role being played by the Bund. When Mr. Manin, a Bundist, tried in *Luch*,[48] to repeat his denial, he was fully exposed by N. Skop (see *Prosveshcheniye* No. 3[49].) But when Mr. Lev. Yurkevich, in *Dzvin* (1913, No. 7-8, p. 92), quotes from *Prosveshcheniye* (No. 3, p. 78) N. Sk.'s statement that "the Bundists together with all the Jewish bourgeois parties and groups have long been advocating cultural-national autonomy" and *distorts* this statement by *dropping* the word "Bundists," and *substituting* the words "national rights" for the words "cultural-national autonomy," one can only raise one's hands in amazement! Mr. Lev Yurkevich is not only a nationalist, not only an astonishing ignoramus in matters concerning the history of the Social-Democrats and their program, but a *downright falsifier of quotations* for the benefit of the Bund. The affairs of the Bund and the Yurkeviches must be in a bad way indeed!

program was supported, not only by Kristan but by the influential Ellenbogen. But it was withdrawn; not a single vote was cast for it. A *territorialist* program was adopted, i. e., one that did *not* create *any* national groups "irrespective of the territory occupied by the members of the nation."

Clause 3 of the adopted program reads: "The self-governing *regions* of one and the same nation shall jointly form a nationally united association, which shall manage its national affairs on an absolutely autonomous basis" (cf. *Prosveshcheniye*, 1913, No. 4, p. 28[51]). Clearly, this compromise program is wrong too. An example will illustrate this. The German working-class suburb of Riga or Lodz, plus the German housing estate near St. Petersburg, etc., would constitute a "nationally united association" of Germans in Russia. Obviously the Social-Democrats cannot *demand* such a thing or *enforce* such an association, although of course they do not in the least deny *freedom* of every kind of association, including associations of any communities of any nationality in a given state. The segregation, by law of the state, of Germans, etc., in different localities and of different classes in Russia into a single German-national association may be practiced by anybody—priests, bourgeois or philistines, but not by Social-Democrats.

5. THE EQUALITY OF NATIONS AND THE RIGHTS OF NATIONAL MINORITIES

When they discuss the national question, opportunists in Russia are given to citing the example of Austria. In my article in *Severnaya Pravda** (No. 10, *Prosveshcheniye*, pp. 96-98), which the opportunists have attacked (Mr. Semkivsky in *Novaya Rabochaya Gazeta*,[52] and Mr. Liebman in *Zeit*), I asserted that, insofar as that is at all possible under capitalism, there was only one solution of the national question, viz., through consistent democracy. In proof of this, I referred, among other things, to Switzerland.

* See pp. 87-89. –*Ed.*

This has not been to the liking of the two opportunists mentioned above, who are trying to refute it or belittle its significance. Kautsky, we are told, said that Switzerland is an exception; Switzerland, if you please, has a special kind of decentralization, a special history, special geographical conditions, unique distribution of a population that speak different languages, etc., etc.

All these are nothing more than attempts to *evade* the issue. To be sure, Switzerland is an exception in that she is not a single-nation state. But Austria and Russia are also exceptions (or are backward, as Kautsky adds). To be sure, it was only, her special, unique historical and social conditions that ensured Switzerland *greater* democracy than most of her European neighbors.

But where does all this come in, if we are speaking of the *model* to be adopted? In the whole world, under present-day conditions, countries in which any particular institution has been founded on *consistent* democratic principles are the exception. Does this prevent us, in our program, from upholding consistent democracy in all institutions?

Switzerland's special features lie in her history, her geographical and other conditions. Russia's special features lie in the strength of her proletariat, which has no precedent in the epoch of bourgeois revolutions, and in her shocking general backwardness, which objectively necessitates an exceptionally rapid and resolute advance, under the threat of all sorts of drawbacks and reverses.

We are evolving a national program from the proletarian standpoint; since when has it been recommended that the worst examples, rather than the best, be taken as a model?

At all events, does it not remain an indisputable and undisputed fact that national peace under capitalism has been achieved (insofar as it is achievable) *exclusively* in countries where consistent democracy prevails?

Since this is indisputable, the opportunists' persistent references to Austria instead of Switzerland are nothing but a typical Cadet device, for the Cadets[53] always copy the worst European constitutions rather than the best.

In Switzerland there are *three* official languages, but bills submitted to a referendum are printed in *five* languages, that is to say, in two Monansh dialects, in addition to the three official languages.

According to the 1900 census, these two dialects are spoken by
38,651 out of the 3,315,443 inhabitants of Switzerland, i.e., by a
little over *one per cent*. In the army, commissioned and non-
commissioned officers "are given the fullest freedom to speak to
the men in their native language." In the cantons of Graubunden
and Wallis (each with a population of a little over a hundred
thousand) both dialects enjoy complete equality.*

The question is: should we advocate and support this, the living
experience of an advanced country, or borrow from the Austrians
inventions like "extra-territorial autonomy," which have not yet
been tried out anywhere in the world (and not yet been adopted
by the Austrians themselves)?

To advocate this invention is to advocate the division of school
education according to nationality, and that is a downright harmful
idea. The experience of Switzerland proves, however, that the
greatest (relative) degree of national peace *can be, and has been,
ensured in practice* where you have a consistent (again relative)
democracy throughout the state.

In Switzerland," say people, who have studied this question, "there is *no national question* in the East-European sense of the term. The very phrase (national
question) is unknown there. . . ." "Switzerland left the struggle between
nationalities a long way behind, in 1797-1803."**

This means that the epoch of the great French Revolution,
which provided the most democratic solution of the current problems of the transition from feudalism to capitalism, *succeeded*
incidentally, *en passant*, in *"solving"* the national question.

Let the Semkovskys, Liebmans, and other opportunists now try
to assert that this "exclusively Swiss" solution is *inapplicable* to any
uyezd or even part of an uyezd in Russia, where out of a population of only 200,000 forty thousand speak *two dialects* and want to
have *complete equality* of language in their area!

Advocacy of complete equality of nations and languages distin-
guishes only the consistently democratic elements in each nation
(i.e., only the proletarians), and *unites* them, not according to nationality, but in a profound and earnest desire to improve the entire system of state. On the contrary, advocacy of "cultural-national
autonomy," despite the pious wishes of individuals and groups,

* See René Henry: *La Suisse et la question des langues*, Berne, 1907.
** See Ed. Blocher: *Die Nationalitäten in der Schweiz*, Berlin, 1910.

divides the nations and in fact draws the workers and the bourgeoisie of any one nation closer together (the adoption of this "cultural-national autonomy" by all the Jewish bourgeois parties).

Guaranteeing the rights of a national minority is inseparably linked up with the principle of complete equality. In my article in *Severnaya Pravda* this principle was expressed in almost the same terms as in the later, official and more accurate decision of the conference of Marxists. That decision demands "the incorporation in the constitution of a fundamental law which shall declare null and void all privileges enjoyed by any one nation and all infringements of the rights of a national minority."

Mr. Liebman tries to ridicule this formula and asks: "Who knows what the rights of a national minority are?" Do these rights, he wants to know, include the right of the minority to have "its own program" for the national schools? How large must the national minority be to have the right to have its own judges, officials, and schools with the instruction in its own language? Mr. Liebman wants it to be inferred from these questions that a "*positive*" national program is essential.

Actually, these questions clearly show what reactionary ideas our Bundist tries to smuggle through under cover of a dispute on supposedly minor details and particulars.

"Its own program" in its national schools! . . . Marxists, my dear nationalist-socialist, have a *general* school program which demands, for example, an absolutely secular school. As far as Marxists are concerned, no *departure* from this general program is anywhere or at any time permissible in a democratic state (the question of introducing any "local" subjects, languages, and so forth into it being decided by the local inhabitants). However, from the principle of "taking educational affairs out of the hands of the state" and placing them under the control of the nations, it ensues that we, the workers, must allow the "nations" in our democratic state to spend the people's money on clerical schools! Without being aware of the fact, Mr. Liebman has clearly demonstrated the reactionary nature of "cultural-national autonomy"!

"How large must a national minority be?" This is not defined even in the Austrian program, of which the Bundists are enamored. It says (more briefly and less clearly than our program does): "The rights of the national minorities are protected by a special law to be passed by the Imperial Parliament" (§4 of the Brünn program).

Why has nobody asked the Austrian Social-Democrats the question: what exactly is that law, and exactly which rights and of which minority is it to protect?

That is because all sensible people understand that it is inappropriate and impossible to define particulars in a program. A program lays down only fundamental principles. In this case the fundamental principle is implied with the Austrians, and directly expressed in the decision of the latest conference of Russian Marxists. That principle is: no national privileges and no national inequality.

Let us take a concrete example to make the point clear to the Bundist. According to the school census of January 18, 1911, St. Petersburg elementary schools under the Ministry of Public "Education" were attended by 48,076 pupils. Of these, 396, i.e., less than one per cent, were Jews. The other figures are: Rumanian pupils—2, Georgians—1, Armenians—3, etc.[54] Is it possible to draw up a "positive" national program that will cover this diversity of relationships and conditions? (And St. Petersburg is, of course, far from being the city with the most mixed population in Russia.) Even such specialists in national "subtleties" as the Bundists would hardly be able to draw up such a program.

And yet, if the constitution of the country contained a fundamental law rendering null and void every measure that infringed the rights of a minority, any citizen would be able to demand the rescinding of orders prohibiting, for example, the hiring, at state expense, of special teachers of Hebrew, Jewish history, and the like, or the provision of state-owned premises for lectures for Jewish, Armenian, or Rumanian children, or even for the one Georgian child. At all events, it is by no means impossible to meet, on the basis of equality, all the reasonable and just wishes of the national minorities, and nobody will say that advocacy of equality is harmful. On the other hand, it would certainly be harmful to advocate division of schools according to nationality, to advocate, for example, special schools for Jewish children in St. Petersburg, and it would be utterly impossible to set up national schools for *every* national minority, for one, two or three children.

Furthermore, it is impossible, in any country-wide law, to define how large a national minority must be to be entitled to special schools, or to special teachers for supplementary subjects, etc.

On the other hand, a country-wide law establishing equality can be worked out in detail and developed through special regulations and the decisions of regional Diets, and town, Zemstvo, village commune and other authorities.

Written in October-December 1913
Published in 1913, in the journal
Prosveshcheniye Nos. 10, 11 and 12
Signed. *V. Ilyin*

Published according to
the journal text

A CONTRIBUTION TO THE HISTORY
OF THE NATIONAL PROGRAM
IN AUSTRIA AND IN RUSSIA

In Austria the national program of the Social-Democratic Party was discussed and adopted at the Brünn Congress in 1899. There is a very widespread but mistaken opinion that this Congress adopted what is known as "cultural-national autonomy." The reverse is true: the latter was *unanimously rejected* there.

The South-Slav Social-Democrats submitted to the Brünn Congress (see p. XV of the official Minutes of the Congress in German) a program of cultural-national autonomy worded as follows:

(§2) "every nation inhabiting Austria, *irrespective of the territory on which its members reside*, shall constitute an autonomous group, which shall quite independently administer all its national (language and cultural) affairs."

The words underlined by us clearly express the *gist* of "cultural-national autonomy" (otherwise called extra-territorial). The state is to perpetuate the delimitation of nations in educational and similar affairs, and every citizen is free to register with any nation he pleases.

At the Congress this program was defended both by Kristan and the influential Ellenbogen. It was later withdrawn, however. Not a single vote was cast for it. Victor Adler, the Party's leader, said, ". . . I doubt whether anybody would at present consider this plan practicable" (p. 82 of the Minutes).

One of the arguments against it, on principle, was advanced by Preussler, who said: "The proposals tabled by comrades Kristan and Ellenbogen would result in chauvinism being perpetuated and introduced into every tiny community, into every tiny group" (*ibid.*, p. 92).

122

Clause 3 of the Brünn Congress program relevant to this subject reads as follows:

"The self-governing *regions* of a given nation shall form a single national association which shall settle all its national affairs quite autonomously."

This is a *territorialist* program which *directly precludes*, for example, *Jewish* cultural-national autonomy. Otto Bauer, the principal theoretician of "cultural-national autonomy," devoted a special chapter of his book (1907) to proving that "cultural-national autonomy" for the Jews could not be demanded.

We would mention on this issue that Marxists stand for full freedom of association, including the association of any national regions (uyezds, volosts, villages, and so forth); but Social-Democrats cannot possibly agree to having statutory *recognition* given to single *national associations* within the state.

In Russia, as it happens, *all* the Jewish bourgeois parties (as well as the Bund, which actually follows in their wake) *adopted* the program of "extra-territorial (cultural-national) autonomy," which was rejected by all the Austrian theoreticians and by the Congress of the Austrian Social-Democratic Party!

This fact, which the Bundists for quite obvious reasons have often tried to deny, can be easily verified by a reference to the well-known book, *Forms of the National Movement* (St. Petersburg, 1910)—see also *Prosveshcheniye* No. 3, 1913.

This fact clearly shows that the more backward and more petty-bourgeois social structure of Russia has resulted in some of the Marxists becoming much more infected with bourgeois nationalism.

The Bund's nationalist vacillations were formally and unequivocally condemned long ago by the *Second* (1903) Congress, which *flatly rejected* the amendment moved by the Bundist Goldblatt on "the setting up of institutions guaranteeing freedom of development for the nationalities" (a pseudonym for "cultural-national autonomy").

When, at the August 1912 Conference of liquidators, the Caucasian Mensheviks, who until then had for decades been strenuously fighting the Bund, themselves slipped into nationalism, under the influence of the entire *nationalist* atmosphere of the counter-revolution, the Bolsheviks *were not the only ones* to condemn them. The Caucasian Mensheviks were also emphatically condemned by the Menshevik Plekhanov, who described their decision as "the adaptation of socialism to nationalism."

"The Caucasian comrades," Plekhanov wrote, "who have begun to talk about cultural autonomy instead of political autonomy, have merely certified the fact that they have unwisely submitted to the hegemony of the Bund."

Besides the Jewish bourgeois parties, the Bund and the liquidators, "cultural-national autonomy" was adopted only by the conference of the petty-bourgeois national parties of the Left-Narodnik trend. But even here four parties (the Jewish Socialist Labor Party; the Byelorussian Hromada; the Dashnaktsutyun and the Georgian Socialists-Federalists[55]), adopted this program, while the two largest parties *abstained from voting*: these were the Russian Left Narodniks and the Polish "Fracy" (P. S. P.)!

The Russian Left Narodniks expressed particular opposition to the *compulsory*, legal-state associations of nationalities proposed in the famous Bund plan.

From this brief historical survey it is clear why both the February and the summer conferences of Marxists in 1913 emphatically condemned the petty-bourgeois and nationalist idea of "cultural-national autonomy."*

Put Pravdy No. 13,
February 5, 1914
Signed: *M*.

Published according to
the text in *Put Pravdy*

---

* See pp. 70-71, also *Collected Works*, Vol. 18, p. 461.—*Ed.*

THE NATIONAL EQUALITY BILL[56]

Comrades:

The Russian Social-Democratic Labor group in the Duma has decided to introduce in the Fourth Duma a Bill to abolish the disabilities of the Jews and other non-Russians. The text of this Bill you will find below.

The Bill aims at abolishing all national restrictions against all nations: Jews, Poles, and so forth. But it deals in particular detail with the restrictions against the Jews. The reason is obvious: no nationality in Russia is so oppressed and persecuted as the Jewish. Anti-Semitism is striking ever deeper root among the propertied classes. The Jewish workers are suffering under a double yoke, both as workers and as Jews. During the past few years, the persecution of the Jews has assumed incredible dimensions. It is sufficient to recall the anti-Jewish pogroms and the Beilis case.

In view of these circumstances, organized Marxists must devote proper attention to the Jewish question.

It goes without saying that the Jewish question can effectively be solved only together with the fundamental issues confronting Russia today. Obviously, we do not look to the nationalist-Purishkevich Fourth Duma to abolish the restrictions against the Jews and other non-Russians. But it is the duty of the working class to make its voice heard. And the voice of the *Russian* workers must be particularly loud in protest against national oppression.

In publishing the text of our Bill, we hope that the Jewish workers, the Polish workers, and the workers of the other oppressed nationalities will express their opinion of it and propose amendments, should they deem it necessary.

At the same time we hope that the Russian workers will give particularly strong support to our Bill by their declarations, etc.

In conformity with Article 4 we shall append to the Bill a special list of regulations and laws to be rescinded. This appendix will cover about a hundred such laws affecting the Jews alone.

A BILL FOR THE ABOLITION
OF ALL DISABILITIES OF THE JEWS
AND OF ALL RESTRICTIONS
ON THE GROUNDS OF ORIGIN OR NATIONALITY

1. Citizens of all nationalities inhabiting Russia are equal before the law.

2. No citizen of Russia, regardless of sex and religion, may be restricted in political or in any other rights on the grounds of origin or nationality.

3. All and any laws, provisional regulations, riders to laws, and so forth, which impose restrictions upon Jews in any sphere of social and political life, are herewith abolished. Article 767, Vol. IX, which states that "Jews are subject to the general laws in all cases *where no special regulations affecting them have been issued*" is herewith repealed. All and any restrictions of the rights of Jews as regards residence and travel, the right to education, the right to state and public employment, electoral rights, military service, the right to purchase and rent real estate in towns, villages, etc., are herewith abolished, and all restrictions of the rights of Jews to engage in the liberal professions, etc., are herewith abolished.

4. To the present law is appended a list of the laws, orders, provisional regulations, etc., that limit the rights of the Jews, and which are subject to repeal.

Put Pravdy No. 48,   Published according to
March 28, 1914   the text in *Put Pravdy*

NATIONAL EQUALITY

In *Put Pravdy* No. 48 (for March 28), the Russian Social-Democratic Labor group in the Duma published the text of its Bill on national equality, or, to quote its official title, "Bill for Abolition of All Disabilities of the Jews and of All Restrictions on the Grounds of Origin or Nationality."*

Amidst the alarms and turmoil of the struggle for existence, for a bare livelihood, the Russian workers cannot and must not forget the yoke of national oppression under which the tens and tens of millions of "subject peoples" inhabiting Russia are groaning. The ruling nation—the Great Russians—constitute about 45 percent of the total population of the Empire. Out of every 100 inhabitants, over 50 belong to "subject peoples."

And the conditions of life of this vast population are even harsher than those of the Russians.

The policy of oppressing nationalities is one of *dividing* nations. At the same time it is a policy of systematic *corruption* of the people's minds. The Black Hundreds' plans are designed to foment antagonism among the different nations, to poison the minds of the ignorant and downtrodden masses. Pick up any Black-Hundred newspaper and you will find that the persecution of non-Russians, the sowing of mutual distrust between the Russian peasant, the Russian petty bourgeois and the Russian artisan on the one hand, and the Jewish, Finnish, Polish, Georgian and Ukrainian peasants, petty bourgeois and artisans on the other, is meat and drink to the whole of this Black-Hundred gang.

But the working class needs *unity, not division*. It has no more bitter enemy than the savage prejudices and superstitions which its enemies sow among the ignorant masses. The oppression of "sub-

---

* See pp. 94-95.—*Ed*.

ject peoples" is a double-edged weapon. It cuts both ways—against the "subject peoples" and against the Russian people.

That is why the working class must protest most strongly against national oppression in any shape and form.

It must counter the agitation of the Black Hundreds, who try to divert its attention to the baiting of non-Russians, by asserting its conviction as to the need for complete equality, for the complete and final rejection of all privileges for any one nation.

The Black Hundreds carry on a particularly venomous hate-campaign against the Jews. The Purishkeviches try to make the Jewish people the scapegoat for all their own sins.

And that is why the R.S.D.L. group in the Duma did right in putting *Jewish* disabilities in the forefront of its Bill.

The schools, the press, the parliamentary rostrum—everything is being used to sow ignorant, savage, and vicious hatred of the Jews.

This dirty and despicable work is undertaken, not only by the scum of the Black Hundreds, but also by reactionary professors, scholars, journalists and members of the Duma. Millions and thousands of millions of rubles are spent on poisoning the minds of the people.

It is a point of honor for the *Russian* workers to have this Bill against national oppression backed by tens of thousands of proletarian signatures and declarations. . . . This will be the best means of consolidating *complete* unity, amalgamating all the workers of Russia, irrespective of nationality.

Put Pravdy No. 62,   Published according to
April 16, 1914   the text in *Put Pravdy*

BILL ON THE EQUALITY OF NATIONS
AND THE SAFEGUARDING OF THE RIGHTS
OF NATIONAL MINORITIES[57]

1. The boundaries of Russia's administrative divisions, rural and urban (villages, volosts, uyezds, gubernias, parts and sections of towns, suburbs, etc.), shall be revised on the basis of a register of present-day economic conditions and the national composition of the population.

2. This register shall be made by commissions elected by the local population on the basis of universal, direct and equal suffrage by secret ballot with proportional representation; national minorities too small (under proportional representation) to elect one commission member shall elect a commission member with a consultative voice.

3. The new boundaries shall be endorsed by the central parliament of the country.

4. Local self-government shall be introduced in all areas of the country without exception, on the basis of universal, direct and equal suffrage by secret ballot with proportional representation; areas with specific geographical, living or economic conditions or a special national composition of the population shall have the right to form autonomous regions with autonomous regional Diets.

5. The limits of jurisdiction exercised by the autonomous Diets and local self-governing bodies shall be determined by the central parliament of the country.

6. All nations in the state are absolutely equal, and all privileges enjoyed by any one nation or any one language are held to be inadmissible and anti-constitutional.

7. The local self-governing bodies and autonomous Diets shall determine the language in which business it to be conducted by state and public establishments in a given area or region, all national minorities having the right to demand absolute safeguards for their language on the basis of the principle of equality, for example, the right to receive replies from state and public establishments in the language in which they are addressed, etc. Measures by Zemstvos, towns, etc., which infringe the equality of languages enjoyed by the national minorities in financial, administrative, legal and all other fields, shall be considered non-valid and subject to repeal on a protest filed by any citizen of the state, regardless of domicile.

8. Each self-governing unit of the state, rural and urban, shall elect, on the basis of universal, direct and equal suffrage by secret ballot with proportional representation, boards of education to take care, wholly and autonomously, of expenditures on all the cultural and educational needs of the population subject to the control and management of the town and Zemstvo bodies.

9. In territorial units with a mixed population the number of members on the boards of education shall not be less than twenty. This number (20) may be increased by order of the self-governing bodies and autonomous Diets. Areas shall be considered as having a mixed population where a national minority constitutes up to five per cent of the population.

10. Every national minority of a given self-governing unit that is too small to elect, under proportional representation, one member of the board of education shall be entitled to elect a member with a consultative voice.

11. The proportional share of the funds expended on the cultural and educational needs of the national minorities in a given area shall not be less than the proportional share of the national minorities in the whole population of the given area.

12. A census of the population, with due account of the native language of citizens, shall be carried out every ten years throughout the state, and every five years in regions and areas with a mixed population.

13. All measures by boards of education which in any way infringe the complete equality of nations and languages of the local population or the proportionality of expenditures on cultural and educational needs in conformity with the share of the national minorities in the population, shall be considered non-valid and subject to repeal on a protest of any citizen of the state, regardless of domicile.

Written after May 6 (19), 1914   Published according to
First published in 1937   the manuscript
in *Lenin Miscellany XXX*

CORRUPTING THE WORKERS
WITH REFINED NATIONALISM

The more strongly the working-class movement develops the more frantic are the attempts by the bourgeoisie and the feudalists to suppress it or break it up. Both these methods—suppression by force and disintegration by bourgeois influence—are constantly employed all over the world, in all countries, and one or another of these methods is adopted alternately by the different parties of the ruling classes.

In Russia, particularly after 1905, when the more intelligent members of the bourgeoisie realized that brute force alone was ineffective, all sorts of "progressive" bourgeois parties and groups have been more and more often resorting to the method of *dividing* the workers by advocating different bourgeois ideas and doctrines designed to weaken the struggle of the working class.

One such idea is refined nationalism, which advocates the division and splitting up of the proletariat on the most plausible and specious pretexts, as for example, that of protecting the interests of "national culture," "national autonomy, or independence," and so on, and so forth.

The class-conscious workers fight hard against *every kind* of nationalism, both the crude, violent, Black-Hundred nationalism, and that most refined nationalism which preaches the equality of nations *together* with . . . the *splitting up* of the workers' cause, the workers' organizations and the working-class movement *according to* nationality. Unlike all the varieties of the nationalist bourgeoisie, the class-conscious workers, carrying out the decisions of the recent (summer 1913) conference of the Marxists, stand, not only for the most complete, consistent and fully applied *equality* of nations and languages, but also for the *amalgamation* of the workers of the different nationalities in *united* proletarian organizations of every kind.

Here lies the fundamental distinction between the national program of Marxism and that of any bourgeoisie, be it the most "advanced."

Recognition of the equality of nations and languages is important to Marxists, not only because they are the most consistent democrats. The interests of proletarian solidarity and comradely unity in the workers' class struggle call for the fullest equality of nations with a view to removing every trace of national distrust, estrangement, suspicion and enmity. And full equality implies the recognition of the *right* of self-determination for all nations.

To the bourgeoisie, however, the demand for national equality very often amounts in practice to advocating national exclusiveness and chauvinism; they very often couple it with *advocacy* of the division and estrangement of nations. This is *absolutely* incompatible with proletarian *internationalism,* which advocates, not only *closer relations* between nations, but the *amalgamation* of the workers of all nationalities in a given state in the *united* proletarian organizations. That is why Marxists emphatically condemn so-called "cultural-national autonomy," i.e. the idea that educational affairs should be *taken out* of the hands of the state and transferred to the *respective* nationalities. This plan means that in questions of "national culture" educational affairs are to be split up in *national associations* according to the nationalities in the given state federation, each with it own *separate* Diet, educational budgets, school boards, and educational institutions.

This is a plan of refined nationalism, which corrupts and divides the working class. To this plan (of the Bundists, liquidators and Narodniks, *i.e.,* of the various petty-bourgeois groups), the Marxists contrapose the principle of complete equality of nations and languages and go to the extent of denying the necessity of an official language; at the same time they advocate the closest possible relations between the nations, uniform *state* institutions for all nations, uniform school boards, a uniform education policy (secular education!, and the unity of the workers of the different nations in the struggle against the *nationalism of every national bourgeoisie,* a nationalism which is presented in the form of the slogan "national culture" for the purpose of deceiving simpletons.

Let the petty-bourgeois nationalists—the Bundists, the liquidators, the Narodniks and the writers for *Dzvin*—openly advocate their principle of refined bourgeois nationalism; that is their right. But they should not try to fool the workers, as Madam V. O.[58] does, for example, in issue No. 25 of *Severnaya Rabochaya Gazeta,* where she assures her readers that *Za Pravdu* is *opposed* to instruction in schools being given in the native languages!

That is gross slander. The Pravdists not only recognize this right, but are *more consistent* in recognizing it than anyone else. The Pravdists, who identified themselves with the conference of Marxists, which declared that *no compulsory official language was necessary,* were the *first* in Russia to recognize *fully* the right to use the native language!

It is crass ignorance to confuse instruction in the native language with "dividing educational affairs within a single state according to nationality," with "cultural-national autonomy," with "taking educational affairs out of the hands of the state."

Nowhere in the world are Marxists (or even democrats) opposed to instruction being conducted in the native language. And *nowhere in the world* have Marxists adopted the program of "cultural-national autonomy"; Austria is the *only* country in which it *was proposed.*

The example of Finland, as quoted by Madam V. O., is an argument against herself, for in that country the *equality of nations and languages* (which we recognize unreservedly and more consistently than anybody) is recognized and carried out, but *there is no question there about taking educational affairs out of the hands of the state,* about separate national associations to deal with all educational affairs, about partitioning up the school system of a country with national barriers, and so forth.

Put Pravdy No. 82,
May 10, 1914
Signed: *V.I.*

Published according to
the text in *Put Pravdy*

LECTURE ON THE 1905
REVOLUTION[59] (Excerpt)

Tsarism vented its hatred particularly upon the Jews. On the one hand, the Jews furnished a particularly high percentage (compared with the total Jewish population) of leaders of the revolutionary movement. And now, too, it should be noted to the credit of the Jews, they furnish a relatively high percentage of internationalists, compared with other nations. On the other hand, tsarism adroitly exploited the basest anti-Jewish prejudices of the most ignorant strata of the population in order to organize, if not to lead directly, *pogroms*—over 4,000 were killed and more than 10,000 mutilated in 100 towns. These atrocious massacres of peaceful Jews, their wives and children roused disgust throughout the civilized world. I have in mind, of course, the disgust of the truly democratic elements of the civilized world, and these are *exclusively* the socialist workers, the proletarians.

Written in German before
January 9 (22),1917
First published in *Pravda*
No. 18,January 22, 1925
Signed: N. Lenin

Published according to
the manuscript
Translated from the German

SPEECHES ON GRAMOPHONE RECORDS[60]

ANTI-JEWISH POGROMS

Anti-Semitism means spreading enmity towards the Jews. When the accursed tsarist monarchy was living its last days it tried to incite ignorant workers and peasants against the Jews. The tsarist police, in alliance with the landowners and the capitalists, organized pogroms against the Jews. The landowners and capitalists tried to divert the hatred of the workers and peasants who were tortured by want against the Jews. In other countries, too, we often see the capitalists fomenting hatred against the Jews in order to blind the workers, to divert their attention from the real enemy of the working people, capital. Hatred towards the Jews persists only in those countries where slavery to the landowners and capitalists has created abysmal ignorance among the workers and peasants. Only the most ignorant and downtrodden people can believe the lies and slander that are spread about the Jews. This is a survival of ancient feudal times, when the priests burned heretics at the stake, when the peasants lived in slavery, and when the people were crushed and inarticulate. This ancient, feudal ignorance is passing away; the eyes of the people are being opened.

It is not the Jews who are the enemies of the working people. The enemies of the workers are the capitalists of all countries. Among the Jews there are working people, and they form the majority. They are our brothers, who, like us, are oppressed by capital; they are our comrades in the struggle for socialism. Among the Jews there are kulaks, exploiters and capitalists, just as there are among the Russians, and among people of all nations. The capitalists strive to sow and foment hatred between workers of different faiths, different nations and different races. Those who do not work are kept in power by the power and strength of capital.

Rich Jews, like rich Russians, and the rich in all countries, are in alliance to oppress, crush, rob and disunite the workers.

Shame on accursed tsarism which tortured and persecuted the Jews. Shame on those who foment hatred towards the Jews, who foment hatred towards other nations.

Long live the fraternal trust and fighting alliance of the workers of all nations in the struggle to overthrow capital.

Recording made at the
end of March, 1919   Published according to
                                                         the gramaphone record

THESES FOR A LECTURE ON
THE NATIONAL QUESTION[61] (Excerpt)

(z*) Jews—mainly traders.

> Sophism of Bundists: we isolate for *pure*
> class struggle.

44. National autonomy for the Jews?
O. Bauer and K. Kautsky. "Caste."
Jewish contribution to world culture and *two*
trends among the Jews.

45. In Russia Jews isolated as a caste.
Way out? (1) freezing isolation in one way or
another
(2) bringing them closer to the
democratic and socialist
movement of the Diaspora countries[62].

> "Expelling the Jews from the ranks of nations". . . . .

46. 10.5 million throughout the world. Two halves

> Asher about Vienna—150,000.

47. *All* bourgeois parties of the Jews have adopted
cultural-national autonomy in Russia

$\left\{ \begin{array}{l} + \text{petty-bourgeois democracy 1907} \\ + \text{Bund?} \qquad (section) \end{array} \right\}$

> What sort of grist has Bauer's (petty-bourgeois,
> opportunist) invention become?

Written between January 10 and 20
(January 23 and February 2), 1914
First published in 1917 in
Lenin Miscellany XXX

Printed from
the original

* Greek letter in the original

APPENDIX

DECLARATION OF THE RIGHTS OF THE NATIONALITIES OF RUSSIA

The October Revolution of the workers and peasants started under the general slogan of freedom.

The peasants have been freed from the rule of the landlords, for large landownership no longer exists—the soil has become free. The soldiers and sailors have been freed from the power of the sovereign generals, for the generals are now elective and removable. The workers have been freed from the caprice and tyranny of the capitalists, for from now on the control of the enterprises and factories by the workers has been established. All that is living and vital has become freed from hated bondage.

Now there remain only the nationalities of Russia, who have suffered and still suffer from oppression and tryanny. Their freedom must immediately be worked for, and it must be brought about resolutely and irrevocably.

During the times of tsarism the nations of Russia were systematically instigated against each other. The results of this policy are known: massacres and pogroms on the one hand, the enslaving of nations on the other hand.

This hideous policy of rousing hatred must and will never return. From now on it will be replaced by the policy of voluntary and honest unions of nations.

In the period of imperialism, after the February Revolution, when political power passed into the hands of the bourgeoisie represented by the Constitutional-Democratic Party, the open policy of instigation was replaced by a policy of cowardly mistrust towards the nations of Russia, a policy of molestation and provocation which was covered with verbose declarations about the "freedom" and "equality" of nations. The results of this policy are known: the sharpening of national enmity, the undermining of mutual trust.

This unworthy policy of lies and mistrust, of molestation and provocation, must be ended. From now on it must be replaced by a frank and honest policy leading to complete mutual trust between the nations in Russia.

Only on the basis of such trust can an honest and firm union of the nations of Russia be formed.

Only on the basis of such a union can the workers and peasants of the nations of Russia be merged into a single revolutionary force, able to withstand all the attacks of the imperialist, annexationist bourgeoisie.

In June of this year the Congress of Soviets proclaimed the free right of self-determination of the nations of Russia.

The second Congress of Soviets, which met in October, even more resolutely and definitely established this inalienable right of the nations of Russia.

Acting on the decisions of this Congress, the Council of People's Commissars plans to base its actions in regard to the nationalities of Russia on the following principles:

1. The equality and sovereignty of the nations of Russia.

2. The right of the nations of Russia to free self-determination including separation and the formation of independent states.

3. The removal of every and any national and national-religious privilege and restriction.

4. The free development of the national minorities and ethnographic groups living within the confines of Russia.

Corresponding concrete provisions will be worked out as soon as the Commission of Nationalities is established.

In the name of the Russian Republic: *Chairman of the Council of People's Commissars*, V. ULYANOV (LENIN); *People's Commissar of Nationalities*, JOSEPH DJUGASHVILI (STALIN).

November 15, 1917.

RESOLUTION OF THE COUNCIL OF PEOPLE'S COMMISSARS
ON THE UPROOTING OF THE ANTI-SEMITIC MOVEMENT

According to reports received by the Council of People's Commissars, the counter-revolutionaries are carrying on agitation for pogroms in many cities especially in the frontier zone, as a result of which there have been sporadic outrages against the toiling Jewish population. The bourgeois counter-revolution has taken up the weapon which has slipped from the hands of the Tsar.

The absolutist government, each time when the need arose, turned the wrath of the peoples directed at itself against the Jews, at the same time telling the uneducated masses that all their misery comes from the Jews. The rich Jews, however, always found a way to protect themselves; only the Jewish poor always suffered and perished from instigation and violence.

The counter-revolutionaries have now renewed hatred against the Jews, using hunger, exhaustion and also the backwardness of the most retarded masses as well as the remnants of that hatred against the Jews which was planted among the people by absolutism.

In the Russian Socialist Federated Soviet Republic, where the principle of self-determination of the toiling masses of all peoples has been proclaimed, there is no room for national oppression. The Jewish bourgeois are our enemies, not as Jews but as bourgeois. The Jewish worker is our brother.

Any kind of hatred against any nation is inadmissible and shameful.

The Council of People's Commissars declares that the anti-Semitic movement and pogroms against the Jews are fatal to the interests of the workers' and peasants' revolution and calls upon the toiling people of Socialist Russia to fight this evil with all the means at their disposal.

National hostility weakens the ranks of our revolutionaries, disrupts the united front of the toilers without distinctions of nationality and helps only our enemies.

The Council of People's Commissars instructs all Soviet deputies to take uncompromising measures to tear the anti-Semitic movement out by the roots. Pogromists and pogrom-agitators are to be placed outside the law.

Chairman of the Council of People's Commissars, ULYANOV (LENIN); *Administrator of Affairs of the Council of People's Commissars,* BONCHE-BUREVICH; *Secretary of the Council,* N. GORBUNOV.

July 27,1918.

NOTES

[1] *Posledniye Izvestia (News)*—a periodical bulletin issued by the Foreign Committee of the Bund from 1901 to 1906.   p. 20

[2] *The Bund* (The General Jewish Workers' Union of Lithuania, Poland, and Russia) came into being in 1897 at the Inaugural Congress of Jewish Social-Democratic groups in Vilna. It consisted mainly of semi-proletarian Jewish artisans of Western Russia. At the First Congress of the R.S.D.L.P. in 1898 the Bund joined the latter "as an autonomous organization, independent only in respect of questions affecting the Jewish proletariat specifically." (*The C.P.S.U. in Resolutions and Decisions of Congresses, Conferences and Plenary Meetings of the Central Committee*, Russ.ed,. Part I, 1954, p. 14.)

The Bund was a vehicle of nationalist and separatist ideas in Russia's working-class movement. In April 1901 the Bund's Fourth Congress resolved to alter the organizational ties with the R.S.D.L.P. as established by the latter's First Congress. In its resolution, the Bund Congress declared that it regarded the R.S.D.L.P. as a federation of national organizations, of which the Bund was a federal member.

Following the rejection by the Second Congress of the R.S.D.L.P. of the Bund's demand for recognition as the sole representative of the Jewish proletariat, the Bund left the Party, but rejoined it in 1906 on the basis of a decision of the Fourth (Unity) Congress.

Within the R.S.D.L.P. the Bund constantly supported the Party's opportunist wing (the Economists, Mensheviks, and liquidators), and waged a struggle against the Bolsheviks and Bolshevism. To the Bolsheviks' programmatic demand for the right of nations to self-determination the Bund contraposed the demand for autonomy of national culture. During the years of the Stolypin reaction and the new revolutionary upsurge, the Bund adopted a liquidationist stand and played an active part in the formation of the August anti-Party bloc. During the First World War (1914-18), the Bundists took a social-chauvinist stand. In 1917 the Bund supported the bourgeois Provisional Government and sided with the enemies of the Great October Socialist Revolution. During the foreign military intervention and the Civil War, the Bundist leaders made common cause with the forces of counter-revolution. At the same time a tendency towards cooperation with the Soviets became apparent among the Bund rank and file. In March 1921 the Bund dissolved itself, part of the membership joining the Russian Communist Party (Bolsheviks) in accordance with the general rules of admission.   p. 20

[3] The reference is to a Yiddish translation of Karl Kautsky's pamphlet, *Social Revolution*.   p. 23

[4] *Hofman*—pseudonym of Bund member V. Kossovsky.   p. 27

[5] This refers to the Northumberland and Durham miners who, in the eighties of the nineteenth century, secured a 7-hour working day for skilled underground workers—through a deal with the coal-owners—but later for a number of years opposed the legal enactment of an 8-hour working day for all workers in Britain.
p.30

[6] The reference is to the Jewish pogrom organized in Kishinev by the tsarist government and the Black Hundreds in April, 1903.   p. 34

[7] *Arakcheyev, A. A.* (1769-1834)—the powerful favorite of Paul I and Alexander I, whose name is associated with a period of crushing police tyranny and jackboot rule.   p. 39

[8] Lenin says that the Central Committee *"has not been born yet"* out of security considerations; actually, the Central Committee already existed—it had been elected at the Second Party Congress on August 7 (20), 1903.   p. 40

[9] The *Arbeiterstimme (Worker's Voice)* was the Central Organ of the Bund; it appeared from 1897 to 1905.   p. 41

[10] The reference is to the decision of the First Congress of the R.S.D.L.P. that the Bund "is affiliated to the Party as an autonomous organization independent only in regard to questions specifically concerning the Jewish proletariat." *The C.P.S.U. in Resolutions and Decisions of Its Congresses, Conferences, and Plenary Meetings of the Central Committee*, 1954, Part I, P. 14.)   p. 41

[11] Mephistopheles' injunction to the student in Goethe's *Faust*.   p. 46

[12] The incident of the Bund's campaign against the Ekaterinoslav Party Committee is described in Lenin's article "Does the Jewish Proletariat Need an 'Independent Political Party'?" (pp. 1-6).   p. 46

[13] *"Tail-ism" (khvostism), "tail-enders"*—expressions originally coined by Lenin to describe the Economists, who denied the leading role of the Party and the importance of theory in the working-class movement; their position implied that the Party should trail after the spontaneously developing movement, follow in the tail of events.   p. 47

[14] *Neue Zeit (New Times)*—the theoretical journal of the German Social-Democratic Party, published in Stuttgart from 1883 to 1923; edited until October 1917 by Karl Kautsky and subsequently by Heinrich Cunow. Some of the works of Marx and Engels were first published in its columns, among them Marx's "Critique of the Gotha Program" (in No. 18 for 1890-91) and Engels "Contribution to the Critique of the Draft Social-Democratic Program" (in No. 1 for 1901-02). While Engels was alive he constantly helped the editors with suggestions and advice, and not infrequently criticized them for departures from Marxism. Contributors included August Bebel, Wilhelm Liebknecht, Rosa Luxemburg, Franz Mehring, Clara Zetkin, G. V. Plekhanov, Paul Lafargue, and other leading figures in the German and international working-class movement of the late nineteenth and early twentieth century. Beginning with the latter half of the nineties, the *Neue Zeit* made a practice of publishing the writings of the revisionists, notably Bernstein's series "Problems of Socialism," which inaugurated the revisionists' campaign against Marxism. During

the First World War it adopted a Centrist, Kautskian position, in effect supporting
the social-chauvinists.   p. 47

15 The quotations are from Alfred Naquet's article "Drumont and Bernard Lazare,"
published on September 24, 1903, in the Paris *La Petite Republique*, at that time
the organ of the French reformist Socialists. The paper was founded in 1875; its
contributors included Jaurès, Millerand, and other well-known personalities. p. 48

16 The *Pale of Settlement* in tsarist Russia was the territory outside, which Jews were
not allowed to live.   p. 48

17 *Ernest Renan* was a prominent French philologist and historian. The quotation is
from his lecture "Judaism as a Race and as a Religion," published in *Discours et
Conférences par Ernest Renan*, Paris, 1887, p. 373.   p. 49

18 *Black Hundreds*—a reactionary, monarchist, pogrom-making organization set up
by the tsarist police to combat the revolutionary movement They murdered revolutionaries, assaulted progressive intellectuals, and organized anti-Jewish
pogroms.   p. 52

19 The document is an editorial preface to the pamphlet *Report on the Third Congress of the R.S.D.L.P.*, published in Yiddish in 1905.   p. 54

20 The decisions here referred to were Draft Terms for the Union of the Bund with
the R.S.D.L.P. (adopted at the Fourth [Unity] Congress of the R.S.D.L.P. in 1906)
and the resolution on "The Unity of National Organizations in the Localities"
(adopted at the Fifth [All-Russian] Conference of the R.S.D.L.P. in 1908). p. 65

21 *Nasha Zarya (Our Dawn)*—a Menshevik liquidator monthly published legally in
St. Petersburg from 1910 to 1914. It served as a rallying center for the liquidationist
forces in Russia.   p. 66

22 Lenin wrote this Draft Platform for the Latvian Bolsheviks in May 1913, when
preparations were being made to convene the Fourth Congress of the Social-
Democrats of the Latvian Area. It was a time when the struggle between the Bolsheviks and Mensheviks in the Latvian Social-Democratic Party had become
sharper; all the central positions in the Party had been seized by Menshevik liquidators and conciliators. The Latvian Bolsheviks formed their group with the
support of Bolshevik-minded workers. Lenin helped them in their struggle against
the liquidationist leadership.
   The Bolshevik leaders of the Latvian Social-Democrats set up their center
abroad—the Bureau of Groups Abroad—and published Lenin's platform as a reprint from No. 8 of their *Bilitens (Bulletin)* under the heading "Our Platform for the
Fourth Congress of Social-Democrats of the Latvian Area." The Draft Platform was
republished in issue No. 9-10 of the *Bilitens*. The editors of the *Bilitens*, influenced
by the conciliatory elements among them, omitted the section of the platform dealing with the national question, and made some alterations and deletions in other
sections.   p. 69

23 The program referred to is the Austrian Social-Democratic Party's Program on
the National Question adopted at the Congress in Brünn (Brno) in September
1899.   p. 71

[24] The publication referred to is *Der Cechoslavische Sozialdemokrat.*   p. 74

[25] These theses were written by Lenin for his lectures on the national question delivered on July 9,10, 11 and 13 (new style), 1913 in the Swiss towns of Zurich, Geneva, Lausanne and Berne.   p. 75

[26] The decisions of the Prague Conference (1912) called the relations that the national Social-Democratic organizations had with the R.S.D.L.P. from 1907 to 1911 *"federation of the worst type."* Although the Social-Democratic organizations of Poland, Lithuania and the Latvian Area, and also the Bund, belonged to the R.S.D.L.P., they actually held themselves aloof. Their representatives did not take part in guiding all-Russian Party work; directly or indirectly they promoted the anti-Party activities of the liquidators. (See *Collected Works,* Vol. 17, pp. 464-65 and Vol. 18, pp. 411-12.)   p. 81

[27] *Russkaya Molva (Russian Tidings)*—a bourgeios daily, organ of the Progressists, founded in 1912. Lenin called the Progressists a mixture of Octobrists and Cadets. The paper appeared in St. Petersburg in 1912 and 1913.   p. 82

[28] *Narodowa Demokracja (National Democracy)*—a reactionary, chauvinist party of the Polish bourgeoisie, founded in 1897. Afraid of the growing revolutionary movement, the party changed its original demand for Polish independence to one for limited autonomy within the framework of the autocracy. During the 1905-07 Revolution, Narodowa Demokracia was the main party of Polish counter-revolution, the Polish Black Hundreds, to use Lenin's expression. They supported the Octobrists in the State Duma.

In 1919 the party changed its name to Zwiazek Ludowo-Narodowy (National-Popular Union) and from 1928 it became the Stronnictwo Narodowe (National Party). After the Second World War, individuals from this party, having no longer any party of their own, attached themselves to Mikolajczyk's reactionary party, the Polske Stronnictwo Ludowe (Polish Popular Party).   p. 82

[29] This refers to the segregation of the schools according to nationality, one of the basic demends of the bourgeois-nationalist program for "cultural-national autonomy."   p. 82

[30] The *Joint Conference of the Central Committee of the R.S.D.L.P. and Party Officials* (for purposes of secrecy it was known as the "Summer" or "August" Conference) was held from September 23 to October 1 (October 6-14), 1913 in the village of Poronin (near Cracow) where Lenin spent the summer months. The Conference was attended by 22 delegates (17 with a vote and 5 with a voice but no vote). Sixteen delegates represented local Party organizations: St. Petersburg——Inessa Armand, A. E. Badayev and A. V. Shotman; Moscow and the Central Industrial Area—F. A. Balashov, Y. T. Novozhilov, R. V. Malinovsky and A. I. Lobov (the two last-named were found to be provocateurs); Ekaterinoslav—G. I. Petrovsky; Kharkov—M. K. Muranov; Kostroma—N. R. Shagov; Kiev—Y. F. Rozmirovich ("Galina"); Urals—S. I. Deryabina ("Sima," "Elena"). Lenin, Krupskaya, Troyanovsky and others represented the Central Committee Bureau Abroad, the central organ of the Party *Sotsial-Demokrat* and the magazine *Prosveshcheniye.* The Bolshevik deputies to the Fourth Duma also represented the Party organizations in the constituencies and towns that elected them to the Duma. Representatives of the Left wing of the Polish Social-Democratic Party, J. S. Hanecky, G. Kamenski ("Domski") and others attended; these delegates had a voice but no vote.

The Conference discussed the following questions: (1) reports from the localities, report on the work of the Polish Social-Democrats, report on the work of the Central Committee; (2) the national question; (3) the work of Social-Democrats in the Duma; (4) the situation in the Social-Democratic Duma group; (5) the question of organization and the Party Congress; (6) the strike movement; (7) work in the legal associations; (8) the Narodniks; (9) the Party press; (10) the forthcoming International Socialist Congress in Vienna. The first two days were devoted to a private conference of the Duma deputies on questions of practical work in the Duma.

Lenin guided the work of the Conference; he opened the meeting with an introductory speech and delivered reports on the work of the Central Committee, the national question and the International Socialist Congress in Vienna; Lenin also spoke on almost all the points of the agenda, made proposals and compiled or edited the draft resolutions.

Reports from the localities told of the growth of the working-class movement. The Conference decided in favor of united All-Russian Party work to guide the actions of the working class on a country-wide scale.

Lenin's report on the Central Committee activity summarized what had been done since the Prague Conference in 1912. In his report on the Vienna International Socialist Congress Lenin proposed sending as many delegates as possible from both legal and illegal organizations, and suggested the holding of a Party congress at the same time as the International Congress. The Conference ended with Lenin's closing speech.

The minutes of the Conference at Poronin have not been found. The resolutions were published as a separate pamphlet under the title *Notification and Resolutions of the Summer, 1913, Joint Conference of the Central Committee of the R.S.D.L.P. and Party Officials,* issued abroad by the Central Committee. For reasons of secrecy some of the resolutions were not printed in full; omitted were point 6 of the resolution on the strike movements and points 1-5 of the resolution on the Party press. The full texts of the resolutions were published illegally in a mimeographed edition.   p. 85

[31] The resolution refers here to the decision adopted by the liquidators' August Conference in 1912 to the effect that "cultural-national autonomy" was compatible with the Program of the R.S.D.L.P.   p. 85

[32] Samoilov made his statement at a session of the State Duma on November 26 (December 9), 1913, during the discussion on a bill to increase the salaries of teachers of religion in agrarian schools.   p. 93

[33] For Lenin's characterization of Peredonov see the article "The Question of Ministry of Education Policy." (*Collected Works,* Vol. 19, p. 143.)   p. 94

[34] The work referred to is Stalin's *Marxism and the National Question.*   p. 95

[35] *Struvism*—a variety of the bourgeois distortion of Marxism.

Struve, B. B.—Russian bourgeois liberal, exponent of legal Marxism in the nineties. He later became one of the leaders of the Cadet Party and after the October Revolution, as a White émigré, was an inveterate enemy of the Soviet Union.   p. 97

[36] This refers to §8 of the Program of the R.S.D.L.P. adopted at the Second Congress of the Party.   p.99

[37] The article "Critical Remarks on the National Question" was written by Lenin in October-December 1913 and published the same year in the Bolshevik legal journal *Prosveshcheniye* Nos. 10, 11 and 12.

The article was preceded by lectures on the national question which Lenin delivered in a number of Swiss cities—Zurich, Geneva, Lausanne and Berne—in the summer of 1913.

In the autumn of 1913 Lenin made a report on the national question at the "August" ("Summer") Conference of the Central Committee of the R.S.D.L.P. with Party workers. A resolution on the report drafted by Lenin was adopted. After the Conference Lenin started work on his article "Critical Remarks on the National Question."   p. 101

[38] *The Black Hundreds*—monarchist gangs formed by the tsarist police to fight the revolutionary movement. They murdered revolutionaries, assaulted progressive intellectuals and organized pogroms.   p. 101

[39] *Russkoye Slovo (Russian Word)*—a daily, published in Moscow from 1895 (the first trial issue appeared in 1894) to July 1918. Formally non-party, the paper defended the interests of the Russian bourgeoisie from a moderate-liberal platform. News was given a wide coverage in the paper, which was the first in Russia to send special correspondents to all the large cities at home and to many foreign capitals.   p. 101

[40] *Purishkevich, V. M.*—(1870-1920)—a big landlord and rabid reactionary (a Black-Hundred monarchist).   p. 103

[41] *Pale of Settlement*—district in tsarist Russia where Jews were permitted permanent residence.   p. 110

[42] *Numerus clausus*—the numerical restriction imposed in tsarist Russia on admission of Jews to the state secondary and higher educational establishments, to employment at factories and offices, and the professions.   p. 110

[43] This refers to the Congress of the Austrian Social-Democratic Party held in Brünn (Austria) from September 24 to 29, 1899 (new style). The national question was the chief item on the agenda. Two resolutions expressing different points of view were submitted to the Congress: (1) the resolution of the Party's Central Committee supporting the idea of the territorial autonomy of nations, and (2) the resolution of the Committee of the South-Slav Social-Democratic Party supporting the idea of extra-territorial cultural-national autonomy.

The Congress unanimously rejected the program of cultural-national autonomy, and adopted a compromise resolution recognizing national autonomy within the boundaries of the Austrian state. (See Lenin's article "A Contribution to the History of the National Program in Austria and in Russia," pp. 91-93.)   p. 113

[44] *J.S.L.P.* (Jewish Socialist Labor Party)—a petty-bourgeois nationalist organization, founded in 1906. Its program was based on the demand for national autonomy for the Jews—the creation of extra-territorial Jewish parliaments authorized to settle questions concerning the political organization of Jews in Russia. The J.S.L.P. stood close to the Socialist-Revolutionaries, with whom it waged a struggle against the R.S.D.L.P.   p. 113

[45] *The Beilis case*—a provocative trial engineered by the tsarist government in 1913

in Kiev. Beilis, a Jew, was falsely accused of having murdered a Christian boy named Yushchinsky for ritual purposes (actually, the murder was organized by the Black Hundreds). The aim of this frame-up was to fan anti-Semitism and incite prgroms so as to divert the masses from the mounting revolutionary movement. The trial excited great public feeling. Workers' protest demonstrations were held in a number of cities. Beilis was acquitted.   p. 114

[46] *Socialist-Revolutionaries*—a petty-bourgeois party in Russia, which came into being at the end of 1901 and beginning of 1902 as a result of a merger of various Narodnik groups and circles. The S.R.s saw no class distinctions between the proletarian and the petty proprietor, played down the class differentiation and antagonisms within the peasantry, and refused to recognize the proletariat's leading role in the revolution. Their views were an eclectic mixture of the ideas of Narodism and revisionism. In Lenin's words, they tried to mend "the rents in the Narodnik ideas with bits of fashionable opportunist 'criticism' of Marxism." (See *Collected Works*, Vol. 9, p. 310.)

The Socialist-Revolutionaries' agrarian program envisaged the abolition of private ownership of the land, which was to be transferred to the village commune on the basis of the "labor principle" and "equalized land tenure," and also the development of cooperatives. This program, which the S.R.s called "socialization of the land," had nothing socialist about it. In his analysis of this program, Lenin showed that the preservation of commodity production and private farming on communal land would not do away with the domination of capital or free the toiling peasantry from exploitation and impoverishment. Neither could the cooperatives be a remedy for the small farmers under capitalism, as they served only to enrich the rural bourgeoisie. At the same time, as Lenin pointed out, the demand for equalized land tenure, though not socialistic, was of a progressive, revolutionary-democratic character, inasmuch as it was directed against reactionary landlordism.

The Bolshevik Party exposed the attempts of the S.R.s to pass themselves off as socialists. It waged a stubborn fight against them for influence over the peasantry, and revealed the damage their tactic of individual terrorism was causing the working-class movement. At the same time, the Bolsheviks, on definite terms, entered into temporary agreements with the Socialist-Revolutionaries to combat tsarism.

The Socialist-Revolutionary Party's political and ideological instability and organizational incohesion, as well as its constant vacillation between the liberal bourgeoisie and the proletariat, were due to the absence of class homogenity among the peasantry. During the first Russian revolution, the Right wing of the S.R.s broke away from the party and formed the legal Labor Popular Socialist Party, whose views were close to those of the Constitutional-Democrats (Cadets), while the Left wing split away and formed a semi-anarchist league of "Maximalists." During the period of the Stolypin reaction, the Socialist-Revolutionary Party suffered a complete breakdown ideologically and organizationally. During the First World War most of its members took a social-chauvinist stand.

After the February bourgeois-democratic revolution of 1917, the Socialist-Revolutionaries, together with the Mensheviks and the Cadets, were the mainstay of the counter-revolutionary Provisional Government of the bourgeoisie and landlords. The leaders of the S.R. Party—Kerensky, Avksentyev and Chernov—were members of this Cabinet. The S.R. Party refused to support the peasants' demand for the abolition of landlordism, and stood for the preservation of landlord ownership. The S.R. members of the Provisional Government authorized punitive action against peasants who had seized landed estates.

At the end of November 1917 the Left wing of the S.R. Party formed an independent party of Left Socialist-Revolutionaries, who, in an endeavor to preserve their influence among the peasant masses, formally recognized Soviet rule and entered into an agreement with Bolsheviks. Shortly, however, they began a struggle against the Soviets.

During the years of foreign intervention and the Civil War the S.R.s carried on counter-revolutionary subversive activities. They actively supported the interventionists and whiteguards, took part in counter-revolutionary plots, and organized terroristic acts against leaders of the Soviet state and the Communist Party. After the Civil War, the S.R.s continued their anti-Soviet activities within the country and in the camp of the White émigrés.   p. 115

[47] *The Polish Socialist Party* (Polska Partia Socjalistyczna)—a reformist nationalist organization founded in 1892. Adopting the slogan of struggle for an independent Poland, the P.S.P., under Pilsudski and his adherents, carried on separatist nationalist propaganda among the Polish workers, whom they tried to divert from the joint struggle with the Russian workers against the autocracy and capitalism. Throughout the history of the P.S.P. Left-wing groups kept springing up within the party, as a result of the activities of the rank-and-file workers. Some of these groups eventually joined the revolutionary wing of the Polish working-class movement.

In 1906 the party split up into the P.S.P. wing and the Right, chauvinist wing (the so-called "revolutionary faction"). Under the influence of the Bolsheviks and the Social-Democratic Party of Poland and Lithuania, the Left wing gradually adopted a consistent revolutionary stand.

During the First World War some of the P.S.P. Left wing adopted an internationalist stand. In December 1918 it united with the Social-Democrats of Poland and Lithuania to form the Communist Workers' Party of Poland (as the Communist Party of Poland was known up to 1925).

During the First World War, the P.S.P. Right wing continued its policy of national chauvinism, organizing Polish legions on the territory of Galicia to fight on the side of Austro-German imperialism. With the formation of the Polish bourgeois state, the Right P.S.P. in 1919 united with the P.S.P. organizations existing on Polish territories formerly seized by Germany and Austria, and resumed the name of the P.S.P. At the head of the government, it arranged for the transfer of power to the Polish bourgeoisie, systematically carried on anti-Communist propaganda, and supported a policy of aggression against the Soviet Union, a policy of conquest and oppression against Western Ukraine and Western Byelorussia. Various groups in the P.S.P. who disagreed with this policy joined the Communist Party of Poland.

After Pilsudski's fascist coup d'état (May 1926), the P.S.P. was nominally a parliamentary opposition, but actually it did not carry on any active fight against the fascist regime, and continued its anti-Communist and anti-Soviet propaganda. During that period the Left-wing elements of the P.S.P. collaborated with the Polish Communists and supported united-front tactics in a number of campaigns.

During the Second World War the P.S.P. again split up. Its reactionary and chauvinist faction, which assumed the name "Wolnosc, Rownosc, Niepodleglosc" (Liberty, Equality, Independence), took part in the reactionary Polish émigré "government" in London. The Left faction, which called itself the Workers' Party of Polish Socialists, under the influence of the Polish Workers' Party, which was founded in 1942, joined the popular front against the Nazi invaders, fought for Poland's liberation, and pursued a policy of friendly relations with the U.S.S.R.

In 1944, after the liberation of Poland's eastern territories and the formation of a Polish Committee of National Liberation, the Workers' Party of Polish Socialists

NOTES   151

resumed the name of P.S.P. and together with the P.S.P. participated in the building up of a people's democratic Poland. In December 1948 the P.W.P. and the
P.S.P. amalgamated and formed the Polish United Workers' Party.   p. 115

[48] *Luch (Ray)*—a legal daily of the Menshevik liquidators, published in St. Petersburg from September 16(29), 1912 to July 5(18), 1913. Put out 237 issues. The
newspaper was maintained chiefly by contributions from the liberals. Ideological
leadership was in the hands of P. B. Axelrod, F. I. Dan, L. Martov, and A. S.
Martynov. The liquidators used the columns of this newspaper to oppose the revolutionary tactics of the Bolsheviks, advocate the opportunist slogan of an "open
party," attack the revolutionary mass strikes of the workers, and attempt to revise
the most important points of the Party Program. Lenin wrote that *Luch* was "en-
slaved by a liberal policy" and called the paper a mouthpiece of the renegades.
                                                                         p. 115

[49] *Prosveshcheniye (Enlightenment)*—a Bolshevik, legal theoretical monthly, published in St. Petersburg from December 1911 to June 1914, with a circulation of up
to five thousand copies.
   The journal was founded on Lenin's initiative to replace the Moscow-published
Mysl, a Bolshevik journal which was closed doen by the tsarist government. Other
workers on the new journal were V. V. Vorovsky, A. I. Ulyanova-Yelizarova, N. K.
Krupskaya and others. Lenin enlisted the services of Maxim Gorky to run the
journal's literary section. Lenin directed *Prosveshsheniye* from Paris and subse-
quently from Cracow and Poronin. He edited articles and regularly corresponded
with the editorial staff. The journal published the following articles by Lenin: "The
Three Sources and Three Component Parts of Marxism," "Critical Remarks on the
National Question," "The Right of Nations to Self-Determination," "Disruption of
Unity Under Cover of Outcries for Unity" and others.
   The journal exposed the opportunists—the liquidators, otzovists, and Trotskyists,
as well as the bourgeois nationalists. It highlighted the struggle of the working class
under conditions of a new revolutionary upsurge, propagandized Bolshevik slogans
in the Fourth Duma election campaign, and came out against revisionism and cen-
trism in the parties of the Second International. The journal played an important
role in the Marxist internationalist education of the advanced workers of Russia.
   On the eve of World War I, *Prosveshcheniye* was closed down by the tsarist
government. It resumed publication in the autumn of 1917, but only one issue (a
double one) appeared, containing Lenin's "Can the Bolsheviks Retain State
Power?" and "A Review of the Party Program."   p. 115

[50] *Bernsteinism*—an anti-Marxist trend in international Social-Democracy. It arose
towards the close of the nineteenth century in Germany and bore the name of the
German opportunist Social-Democrat Eduard Bernstein. After the death of F. Engels, Bernstein publicly advocated revision of Marx's revolutionary theory in the
spirit of bourgeois liberalism (see his article "Problems of Socialism" and his book
The Premises of Socialism and the Tasks of Social-Democracy) in an attempt to
convert the Social-Democratic Party into a petty-bourgeois party of social reforms.
In Russia this trend was represented by the "legal Marxists," the Economists, the
Bundists, and the Mensheviks.   p. 115

[51] Lenin refers to Stalin's article "Marxism and the National Question" published in
the legal Bolshevik journal *Prosveshcheniye*, Nos. 3, 4 and 5 for 1913 under the title
"The National Question and Social-Democracy." Chapter 4 of Stalin's article quotes

the text of the national program adopted at the Brünn Congress of the Austrian
Social-Democratic Party.   p. 116

[52] *Novaya Rabochaya Gazeta (New Workers' Paper)*—a legal daily for the Menshevik liquidators, published in St. Petersburg from August 1913. From January 30
(February 12), 1914 it was superceded by *Severnaya Rabochaya Gazeta (Northern
Workers' Paper)* Lenin repeatedly referred to this newspaper as the *Novaya Lik-
vidatorskaya Gazeta (New Liquidationist Paper)*.   p. 116

[53] *Cadets*—members of the Constitutional-Democratic Party, the principal party of
the liberal-monarchist bourgeoisie in Russia. It was formed in October 1905 and
consisted of representatives of the bourgeoisie, landlord members of the Zemstvos,
and bourgeois intellectuals. Prominent leaders of the Cadets were: P. N. Milyukov,
S. A. Muromtsev, V. A. Maklakov, A. I. Shingaryov, P. B. Struve and F. I.
Rodichev. To mislead the masses the Cadets called themselves the "party of
people's freedom," but actually they went no further than the demand for a constitutional monarchy. They considered the fight against the revolutionary movement their chief aim, and strove to share power with the tsar and the feudalist
landlords. During World World War I the Cadets actively supported the tsarist
government's aggressive foreign policy, and during the February 1917 bourgeois-
democratic revolution they tried to save the monarchy. Holding key posts in the
bourgeois Provisional Government, the Cadets pursued an anti-popular and
counter-revolutionary policy. After the victory of the October Socialist Revolution,
the Cadets came out as the avowed enemies of Soviet rule, taking part in all armed
counter-revolutionary acts and campaigns of the interventionists. Living abroad as
émigrés after the defeat of the interventionists and whiteguards, the Cadets continued their anti-Soviet activities.   p. 117

[54] Lenin obtained these figures from the statistical handbook *One-Day Census of
Elementary Schools in the Empire, Made on January 18, 1911. Issue I, Part 2, St.
Petersburg Educational Area. Gubernias of Archangel, Vologda, Novgorod, Olon-
ers, Pslov and St. Petersburg.* St. Petersburg, 1912, p. 72.   p. 120

[55] The reference is to *Byelorussian Socialist Hromada*—a nationalist organization
which came into being in 1902 under the name of "Byelorussian Revolutionary
Hromada." It defended the interests of the Byelorussian bourgeoisie, landlords and
kulaks, denied the revolutionary class struggle, and tried to keep the Byelorussian
people away from the Russian revolutionary working class. These attempts met with
no support among the working masses of the Byelorussian people. In the national
question, the Hromada stood for "cultural-national autonomy." After the February
bourgeois-democratic revolution of 1917 the Hromada supported the policy of the
bourgeois Provisional Government. Following the October Socialist Revolution it
split up into three counter-revolutionary groups who joined the whiteguards and
foreign interventionists in an active struggle against the Soviets.

Dashnaktsutyun—a bourgeois-nationalist party founded in the early nineties of
the nineteenth century in Turkish Armenia with the aim of liberating the Armenians from the Turkish yoke. The party was a bourgeois-democratic conglomerate of
representatives of various classes. Alongside the bourgeoisie, a prominent place in
it was occupied by the national intelligentsia, as well as by peasants and workers
unaffected by Social Democratic propaganda, and part of the lumpenproletariat
forming the zinvors squads.

On the eve of the 1905-07 Revolution this party transferred its activities to the

Caucasus and aligned itself with the Socialist-Revolutionaries. The party's Left wing formed the young Dashnaktsutyun group, which joined the S. R. Party in 1907.

The activities of the Dashnaktsutyun were of an anti-popular nature. Its nationalist propaganda was greatly detrimental to the internationalist education of the proletariat and the masses of Armenia and the entire Transcaucasia.

After the February bourgeois-democratic revolution of 1917, the Dashnaks supported the policy of the bourgeois Provisional Government. After the October Socialist Revolution they entered into a counter-revolutionary bloc with the Mensheviks, S. R.s and Musavatists against the Bolsheviks. In 1918-20 the Dashnaks stood at the head of the bourgeois-nationalist counter-revolutionary government of Armenia. Their action was designed to convert Armenia into a colony of the foreign imperialists and a stronghold of the Anglo-French interventionists and Russian whiteguards in their struggle against the Soviet government. Under the leadership of the Bolshevik Party and with the help of the Red Army, the working people of Armenia overthrew the Dashnak government in November 1920. With the victory of the Soviets, the Dashnaktsutyun organizations in Transcaucasia were smashed and liquidated.

Georgian Socialists-Federalists—a bourgeois-nationalist party founded in April 1904. Demanded national autonomy for Georgia within the framework of the Russian bourgeois-landlord state. During the period of reaction, the Socialists-Federalists became open opponents of the revolution. In concert with the Mensheviks and anarchists, this party tried to smash the united international front of the working people of Transcaucasia against tsarism and capitalism. After the Great October Socialist Revolution the S. F.s, together with the Georgian Mensheviks, the Dashnaks and Musavatists, organized a counter-revolutionary bloc, which was supported by the Germano-Turkish and later by the Anglo-French interventionists.   p. 124

⁵⁶ *The National Equality Bill* (official title of the "Bill for the Abolition of all Disabilities of the Jews and of all Restrictions on the Grounds of Origin or Nationality") was drafted by Lenin for the Russian Social-Democratic Labor group in the Fourth Duma, apparently in connection with the discussion of the Ministry of the Interior's budget.

In publishing this Bill of the R.S.D.L. group, Lenin considered it a point of honor on the part of the Russian workers to support it with tens of thousands of signatures and declarations. "This," said Lenin, "will be the best means of consolidating *complete* unity, amalgamating all the workers of Russia, irrespective of nationality." (See the article "National Equality," pp. 96-97.)   p. 125

⁵⁷ *Bill on the Equality of Nations and the Safeguarding of the Rights of National Minorities* was drafted by Lenin for introduction in the Fourth Duma by the Bolshevik group.

The plan of the Bill was outlined in a letter to S. G. Shahumyan, dated May 6(19), 1914, from Lenin who attached special importance to the introduction of this Bill in the Duma. "In this way," he wrote, "I believe we can popularly explain the stupidity of cultural-national autonomy and *crush* the votaries of this folly once for all."

The Bill was not introduced.   p. 129

⁵⁸ V. O.—author of the article "The Deterioration of School Education" published in *Severnaya Rabochaya Gazeta* No. 35, March 21, 1914.   p. 133

[59] The *Lecture on the 1905 Revolution* was delivered in German on January 9 (22), 1917 at a meeting of young workers in the Zurich People's House. Lenin began working on the lecture in the closing days of 1916. He referred to the lecture in a letter to V. A. Karpinsky dated December 7 (20), asking for literature on the subject.   p. 134

[60] The making of gramophone records of Lenin's speeches was organized by *Tsentropechat* (the central agency of the All-Russia Central Executive Committee for the Supply and Distribution of Periodicals). Between 1919 and 1921, 13 of Lenin's speeches were recorded.   p. 135

[61] The theses were apparently written by Lenin after his lecture in Paris on January 10(23), 1914 (see *Lenin Miscellany XXX*, pp. 51-57). The inscription on the cover of the "National Question III" notebook is an indication that Lenin repeated his Paris lecture at Liege on February 2, 1914.   p. 137

[62] *Diaspora* (Gk. for dispersal)—the Jews living outside Judea. In the early 6th century B.C., there were Jewish communities in Egypt, Babylon and other countries of the Mediterranean. From the 3rd century B.C., the Diaspora grew rapidly, so that in the 1st century B.C., their number came to 4.5 million. In the Roman Empire, the Jews lived in communities, sometimes forming public-law corporations (as in Alexandria), or private religious societies (as in Rome). On the one hand, the Jews of the Diaspora successfully conducted the propaganda of Judaism, and on the other, they were gradually losing their national traits and language.   p. 137

ABOUT THE EDITOR

DR. HYMAN LUMER was born in Brooklyn, N.Y. in 1909. He began his career as a biologist, earning his Ph.D. in that subject at Western Reserve University in Cleveland in 1935. He later taught the subject there, and at Fenn College, also in Cleveland, where he headed the biology department. He has written numerous research articles in the field of biology.

After leaving Fenn College in 1947, he served as Educational Director of the Ohio-Kentucky district of the United Electrical, Radio and Machine Workers Union until 1950.

In the 1950s he was prosecuted under the anti-Communist section of the infamous Taft-Hartley Act, and served a prison sentence as a result.

He served for many years as the National Educational Director of the Communist Party and is presently the Editor of its monthly theoretical journal *Political Affairs*.

Other books written by Dr. Lumer are:

Zionism: Its Role in World Affairs (1973)
Is Full Employment Possible? (1962)
Poverty: Its Roots and Future (1955)